Nine Steps to Law School Success

Nine Steps to Law School Success

A Scientifically Proven Study Process
for Success in Law School

Lisa M. Blasser

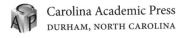

Carolina Academic Press

DURHAM, NORTH CAROLINA

Library of Congress Cataloging-in-Publication Data

Names: Blasser, Lisa M., author.
Title: Nine steps to law school success : a scientifically proven study process
    for success in law school / by Lisa M. Blasser.
Description: Durham, North Carolina : Carolina Academic Press, LLC, [2020]
Identifiers: LCCN 2020041678 (print) | LCCN 2020041679 (ebook) |
    ISBN 9781531000370 (paperback) | ISBN 9781531000387 (ebook)
Subjects: LCSH: Law--Study and teaching--United States. |
    Law schools--United States.
Classification: LCC KF272 .B53 2020 (print) | LCC KF272 (ebook) |
    DDC 340.071/173--dc23
LC record available at https://lccn.loc.gov/2020041678
LC ebook record available at https://lccn.loc.gov/2020041679

Carolina Academic Press
700 Kent Street
Durham, North Carolina 27701
Telephone (919) 489-7486
Fax (919) 493-5668
www.cap-press.com

I dedicate this book to my very best friend — my husband, my rock — Billy, and our two perfect miracles. You three (and Clyde and Elvis, of course) are the proof positive that everything in life is possible, *and more*. I choose you three, every time, without fail, over and over.

Contents

STEP 3

STEP 4

STEP 5

Acknowledgments

Thank you, Mom and Wayne, for relentlessly supporting my heart and for teaching me that in life, *everything is possible.* Mom, you are my angel walking this earth alongside me. Thank you to my dearest Pops, for challenging me to be the greatest version of myself, which has given me boundless drive to succeed in everything I attempt in this beautiful life you provided me. Thank you to my three siblings, Gina, Tony and Joey, for genuinely supporting this book and my dreams — I am profoundly grateful to be in each other's corners.

Thank you also to Michael H. Schwartz for the idea of conducting this qualitative phenomenological study and to my close academic support colleagues who inspire me and share a deep passion for helping students succeed in law school.

Introduction

Some believe that you need to be "super smart" to succeed in law school. This book, however, scientifically proves that grit is the crucial key to flourishing in law school. If you are capable of following a rigorous study process, you can and will succeed in law school.

There are tons of books and articles on the topic of preparing students to be successful in law school. While you may have heard this before, this book is different than the rest. Really, it is! *Nine Steps to Law School Success* ("*Nine Steps*") is the first and only book in legal education to present a *scientifically proven study process for success in law school.* The result of an empirical study, the successful law school study process is based on unbiased information received from the combined experiences of real, current, successful law students in the middle of their law school career. The outcome is a linear, chronological, straightforward study process for you to complete before and during law school, as you lead up to your final exams.

While some students may take the initiative to complete the study steps on their own, the data gathered in *Nine Steps* offers law students a system to motivate themselves to complete the study steps. *Nine Steps* uncovers that drive is critical to success is law school — and this book is the first of its kind to provide both the process to succeed as well as the forces that will encourage you to succeed in law school.

Nine Steps does not inundate you with scholarly opinions from experts, prejudiced perspectives from professors, war stories from recent law school graduates, tales from hardened practitioners or difficult to understand learning theory. The aforementioned, while incredibly important on their own, convolute the simplicity of the scientific study process necessary to achieve success in law school. With all of the work and anticipation leading up to starting law school, what you need is a verified, quick guide of what to do, when to do it and a reward system for when you execute each step to keep you going. That's exactly what you get with *Nine Steps*.

Since law rarely intersects with science, Chapter 1 introduces into the law school realm the qualitative phenomenological study, which was the scientific approach used to uncover the successful law school study process.

Chapter 2 presents the study results in nine steps. Each step is accompanied by the successful law students' explanation of how they are motivated to complete each step in the study process by achieving (1) an understanding of course material, and (2) ultimate success in the course. These explanations are the true forces that compel successful law students to engage in the study process. Some steps also contain examples for a quick visual on how to complete the step as well as a "quick tip" about the step from the author.

Chapter 3 describes how to implement the nine study steps into a weekly schedule so you can either hit the ground running the week before you begin your law school career or implement the process at any stage of your law school career.

Chapter 4 stresses the importance of setting realistic study goals to succeed in law school.

Although *Nine Steps* is based on the law school study process, Chapter 1 can be used as a template for anyone who wishes to conduct a scientific study to uncover a phenomenon in their personal or professional life. To encourage more law students, law professors and lawyers to engage in qualitative research to uncover, rather than hypothesize about, phenomena occurring in law school or the practice, this book spends an entire chapter providing a template for and data from the science supporting the successful law school study process. The good news is that if you are not interested in the science, you can skip to the goods — the research results — in Chapter 2, confident that you are receiving an evidence-based, successful, law school study process.

Nine Steps is intended for anyone capable of fully investing and dedicating themselves to a process that leads to success in law school, including pre-law undergraduates, incoming 1L law students and current law students who may be struggling to succeed in law school or on academic probation in law school. No matter what your incoming law school credentials and qualifications may be, this book will help you achieve success to your maximum level.

Success in law school is not a mistake; it is the result of a fully executed study process that is executed with passion. Since success is not a fixed trait (and our brains crave learning), anyone can achieve it. Now, go get it. I believe in you!

Nine Steps to Law School Success

CHAPTER ONE

The Science behind *Nine Steps*

Why Is a Scientific Study Necessary?

What must you do to succeed in law school? The million-dollar question.

Former law students, lawyers and law professors know the answer to this question. But the idiosyncratic study process of one person is not necessarily the study process that will work for every law student across the board. Even when students share a common goal of wanting to succeed in law school, each student analyzes and comprehends substance in a different manner and carries out different means to achieve their ends. In light of this, I wanted to do something more than simply answer the million-dollar question by authoring a book based on my opinion and experience with studying in law school. I wanted to provide a comprehensive study process straight from the mouths of successful law students.

Incoming Law Students Need a Proven Study Process

For incoming 1L students, the law school study process is foreign. Even if the incoming student is aware that they need a study process, it is not something that comes naturally to students because the law school study process is unlike any other experience they have had previously.

Current Law Students Need a Proven Study Process

Current law students sometimes come to my office baffled that they failed a course or received a lower grade than they felt they deserved. In trying to find the metaphorical needle in their haystack causing them to struggle, I spent a lot of time asking students about the study process, or lack thereof, that they employed before the final exam. It was typical to find major fractures in their processes. Office hours became more of a fishing expedition and by the time we began to scratch the surface of their study weaknesses, the meeting was over, and it was time for the next student, and the next student, etc. Instead of leaving our meeting with a fresh plan on how to succeed, students sometimes left my office with an understanding of their weaknesses, which left me unsatisfied.

I knew the students' confusion or poor grades stemmed from a lack of a formal study process, which resulted in them wasting time doing duplicative tasks, having a lack of understanding of all of the topics they were responsible for learning, disorganized essay writing and struggles with time management.

Also troubling was that we lacked a common language to reference skills students were completing (and failing to complete) while studying, making it difficult to understand the chronology of how or what the student actually studied. For example, I may ask a student, "Did you create a topic outline or topic approach before writing a practice hypothetical?" The student might be clueless about the particular skill I was referencing or mistake the skill for some other skill. We spent a lot of wasted time defining the things students were doing to study.

It was apparent I needed a better platform to communicate the steps necessary to succeed in law school. We needed (and I suspected students at other law schools could benefit from) a linear process of simple study steps to follow. A process that provided a common discourse for students to discuss the skills involved in studying with their professors and one another. One that motivated students to do the work. But what were those exact steps, why would they help students succeed in law school and how could I motivate students to do the steps?

I found an answer to that last compound question. *What if I were to tell you that there indeed exists one study process you can employ to succeed in law school?* Would you do it? If so, the qualitative phenomenological study, which is the foundation of this book, is your answer. The study results explain the phenomenon of what needs to be done to succeed in law school. The data has also been interpreted to explain why those study steps are crucial in motivating law students to do the work.

Personal Reason for Conducting the Scientific Study

When I was a law student, I wish someone would have given me a study process to follow. I was taught the definition of study skills like case briefing and essay writing, but I was never taught the succession of when to complete the study skills. This led me to study in an unorganized manner, and I viewed each skill separately in a vacuum. I was putting in sixty-hour study weeks, *but I was failing out of law school.* After my second semester, I was placed on academic probation. I had to figure out why my studying did not equate to success. One professor unfortunately mistook my poor grades as a lack of effort, which frustrated me to my core because I did not lack grit, I simply did not understand the course material. That was it! In that moment of sobbing in my professor's office out of sheer exasperation for being labeled lazy and feeling stupid I realized I had to figure out why I did not understand my course material. What was I doing?

I went home and cleared everything off my sweet IKEA desk. I started over from the beginning, documenting my study steps. Once the steps were clear, *I knew how to study because each step was intentional, and I understood why each step was necessary.* From then on, I wore my poor academic standing as a badge of inspiration to prove I was neither lazy nor stupid. I told every peer and professor that I was on probation. Using my study process increased my grades every successive semester, and I ultimately graduated with honors and passed the California Bar Exam on my first attempt. I kept the academic probation notice letter in my glove box during law school and now it is framed on the wall of my law practice office that I co-founded, own and manage, right next to my Juris Doctorate and my beautiful license to practice law.

When I became a law professor, I was on a mission to give students a study process (and also to never assume students were lazy or stupid). To my surprise, there were still numerous fantastic books that defined law school skills, but I was unable to find a book that provided a step-by-step chronological law school study process. How could that be? I attended a national conference and told an academic support colleague, Michael H. Schwartz, about my conundrum of not finding a source on point and my idea to write a book about the study process I employed in law school so others could use it to succeed. He replied, "You should conduct a study that proves what the successful study process is as opposed to telling students to follow your own." The rest is history.

When I started researching which scientific method to use, I could not find any scientific study on the law school study process. In fact, I only found one qualitative study done in the entirety of legal education. Since I learned so much from my study, it is my hope that presenting the detailed process of how my scientific research was conducted will afford other law students, law professors, judges, juries, lawyers — or anyone who wants to uncover a phenomenon — with a simple qualitative research template to follow and, perhaps, lead them to pursue their own empirical research in the legal field and beyond.

What Can You Expect from *Nine Steps*?

Since qualitative research has rarely been conducted in legal education and never before on the topic of the successful law school study process, Chapter 1 starts with a quick introduction to empirical research and then discusses the particular qualitative phenomenological method used to unearth the successful law school study process. Chapter 2 reveals the results of the study. Chapter 3 explains how to implement the successful study process into a weekly schedule. Finally, Chapter 4 challenges you to set realistic study goals in law school.

If you are not at all interested in the science backing the results of this study and instead prefer to just get your hands on the successful law school study process, skip ahead to Chapters 2, 3 and 4 (and no offense taken, I promise).

A. The Qualitative Phenomenological Study on What Students Do to Succeed in Law School

When conducting an empirical study, the researcher must first decide which scientific approach to use and then which specific methodology within that approach to execute. During the study, the researcher selects research participants and collects and interprets data from each participant. After the study is completed, the researcher writes a composite summary of the data, transforming the participants' words into scientific meaning to support the research. What remains are certain themes throughout the data, and the researcher then must discover and interpret the meaning of those themes.

A visual of the empirical study process for qualitative phenomenological research (the method used in this book) is provided in Table 1 as an overview and discussed in detail thereafter:

Table 1: Visual of Qualitative Phenomenological Research Scheme

Pick Your Scientific Approach:

1. Qualitative
2. Quantitative

If You Pick the Qualitative Approach, Pick Your Scientific Methodology:

1. Phenomenological
2. Ethnography
3. Grounded-Theory
4. Narrative Research
5. Case Study

If You Pick the Phenomenological Method:

1. Select Research Participants
2. Collect Study Data
3. Interpret Study Data
4. Write a Composite Summary of the Data
5. Discover and Interpret the Data Themes

Participant Sampling Techniques:

1. Convenience Sample
2. Theoretical Sample
3. Judgment Sample

Data Collection Methods:

1. Interview
2. Observation
3. Written Documents

i. Qualitative versus Quantitative Approaches

There are two broad empirical approaches to collecting data: quantitative research and qualitative research. Quantitative researchers use experiments and surveys to gather data in numbers, which are then put into categories or units of measurement. Qualitative researchers use observation and interviews to study things in their natural environment, trying to make sense of phenomena in terms of the meanings people bring to them.

While quantitative research can tell the number of people that feel a certain way, qualitative research explains *the reason people feel a certain way.* That is, the goal of qualitative research is to better understand human behavior, to grasp the process by which people construct the meaning of things in their lives and to describe what those meanings are.

Early on in my research, it became clear that if I want to understand the complexity of human behavior that law students describe as essential to success in law school, a qualitative study was necessary. I had to interview successful law students and make sense of their study processes.

After selecting the qualitative approach, the next step in my study was to select the appropriate qualitative method to conduct my research.

ii. Qualitative Research Methods

One of the first books devoted to qualitative research methods, *Qualitative Research for Education*, was written by Robert Bogdan and Sari Bilken in 1982. Since then, there has been an eruption of information defining the various methods used when conducting qualitative research, almost too much to absorb.

John W. Creswell's, *Qualitative Inquiry and Research Design: Choosing Among Five Traditions*, focuses on the five traditional methods for conducting qualitative research.[1] Each method described in Creswell's original book and subsequent editions has remained largely consistent from 1987 to present.[2] Creswell's methods have never been implemented in a qualitative study on legal education until *Nine Steps.*

---

1. The five traditional qualitative methods are the phenomenological method, the ethnography method, the grounded theory method, the narrative research method and the case study method. There also exist several other non-traditional methods for conducting qualitative research, which are not listed here.

2. John W. Creswell, Research Design: Qualitative and Quantitative Approaches, (3rd Edition, 2013), p. 10.

To determine which method would yield the most comprehensive experience of the successful study process, all five of Creswell's qualitative methods were considered in detail. Since the goal of my study was to uncover an unknown event (the successful law school study process), one method clearly emerged as the appropriate method to conduct this qualitative study: the phenomenological method.

Phenomenology originates in traditions that evolved over centuries; however, most historians credit Edmund Husserl for defining phenomenology in the early twentieth century.[3] Phenomenology is about understanding how human beings experience their world.[4] It gives researchers a powerful tool to understand a subjective experience.[5] In other words, two people may have the same diagnosis with the same treatment prescribed, but the ways in which they experience that diagnosis and treatment will be different, even though they may have some experiences in common.[6] Phenomenology helps researchers to explore those experiences, thoughts and feelings and helps to elicit the meaning underlying how people behave.[7]

After selecting the phenomenological method, the next step in my study was to conduct research to uncover the perspectives of successful law students and their study process.

iii. The Qualitative Phenomenological Exploration of a Law Student's Successful Study Process

The next three steps in the research scheme were critical to uncovering the phenomenon of the successful law school study process: (1) selecting research participants; (2) collecting the study data; and (3) interpreting the collected data.

1. Selection of Research Participants

Qualitative researchers recognize that some informants are "richer" than others and that these people are more likely to provide insight and understand-

---

3. Neubauer, B.E., Witkop, C.T. & Varpio, L. How Phenomenology Can Help Us Learn from the Experiences of Others, Perspect Med. Educ. 8, 90 (2019).

4. Zubin Austin and Jane Sutton, Qualitative Research: Getting Started, (The Canadian Journal of Hospital Pharmacy, 2014), p. 1.

5. *Id.*

6. *Id.*

7. *Id.*

ing for the researcher.[8] Choosing someone at random to answer a qualitative question would be analogous to randomly asking a passer-by how to repair a broken down car, rather than asking a garage mechanic — the former might have a good stab, but asking the latter is likely to be more productive.[9]

There are three broad techniques to selecting a sample for a qualitative study: a convenience sample, a theoretical sample and a judgment sample.[10]

A judgment sample is the most common sampling technique, where the researcher actively selects the most productive sample to answer the research question.[11] This can involve developing a framework of the variables that might influence an individual's contribution and is based on the researcher's practical knowledge of the research area, the available literature and evidence from the study itself.[12]

The sampling technique used in my study was judgment sampling. Successful law students possess knowledge and experience about the process they undertake from the beginning of the semester through taking the final examination. Therefore, I needed to engage with successful law students — apprentices who would produce the most relevant information to my research question — to collect data regarding their experience with studying in law school.

I solicited participants by emailing all 2L, 3L and 4L students (the 4L students were in a part-time program) who had a cumulative grade point average of 2.7 and above.[13] I explained that I was conducting research on the process of studying and requested volunteers to interview about their study process.

---

8. Marshall, MN., *Sampling for Qualitative Research*, 13 Family Practice 522, 523 (1996), available at http://spa.hust.edu.cn/2008/uploadfile/2009-9/2009091622153945.pdf.

9. *Id.*

10. A convenience sample is the least rigorous technique, involving the selection of the most accessible subjects — it is the least costly to the researcher, in terms of time, effort and money, but may result in poor quality data and lacks intellectual credibility. *Id.* Theoretical sampling necessitates building interpretative theories from the emerging data and selecting a new sample to examine and elaborate on this theory. *Id.*

11. *Id.*

12. *Id.*

13. For purposes of this study, I defined a "successful law student" as a current Western State College of Law student who possessed, at the time of the interview, a cumulative law school grade point average of 2.7 or above and a minimum of 30 units of instruction. The 2.7 mark is the cutoff to interview for a prestigious Dean's Fellow position at Western State College of Law and it is also two tenths of a point above the grade point average that the Western State College of Law faculty and administration collectively agree as the grade point necessary for success in law school, on the bar exam and in the practice of law.

Several students responded and, to ensure no bias, I scheduled interviews in the order which they responded.

After completing five interviews with successful students, similar data trends started to emerge. After completing seven interviews, no new explanations emerged, so one more interview was conducted to confirm that I achieved data saturation. The eighth interview confirmed data saturation, warranting a cancellation of the remaining interviews.

Does it surprise you that this book is based on the study process of *only* eight successful law students? For some it may; however, data saturation is not dependent on the amount of data collected but based on the richness of the emerging data set.[14] There is some controversy, though, as to whether it is really possible to achieve true data "redundancy" or saturation, because further interviews always have the potential to uncover something new or unexpected.[15] Therefore, the point at which this situation seems to occur will vary with each study and cannot be predicted. However, once the researcher is reasonably satisfied that heir point has potentially been achieved, data collection can then cease, and the researcher can move on to the next stage in the research process — data analysis.[16]

Of the eight students interviewed, four were male and four were female. The average age of the participants was 29, the youngest being 24 and the oldest being 48. Two students were former students of my Introduction to Legal Skills course, two were former students who had been successful in getting off academic probation, two students worked with me in their capacity as a dean's fellows and I had never worked with or taught the other two students prior to this study.

Table 2 summarizes the background of my study participants.

---

14. Violeta Lopez and Dean Whitehead, *Sampling Data and Data Collection in Qualitative Research*, Nursing and Mid-Wifery Research (4th Ed.), page 136, (citing Tuckett 2004; Guest et al. 2006).

15. *Id.,* citing Wray et al., 2007.

16. Violeta Lopez and Dean Whitehead, *Sampling Data and Data Collection in Qualitative Research*, Nursing and Mid-Wifery Research (4th Ed.), page 136.

Table 2: Background of Study Participants

STUDENT[17]	AGE	GENDER	UNDERGRAD INSTITUTION	UNDER-GRAD GPA	LAW SCHOOL STATUS	LAW SCHOOL CUM. GPA
Antonio[18]	24	Male	Cal Poly Pomona	3.4	3L Full-Time	3.4
Bari[19]	48	Male	Harvard University & UCLA Med. School	3.5 3.8	2L Part-Time	3.9
Carlota[20]	25	Female	Biola University	3.5	3L Full-Time	3.0
Denzel[21]	28	Male	U.C. Irvine	2.0	2L Full-Time	3.5
Ester[22]	25	Female	Cal Poly Pomona	2.8	3L Full-Time	2.8
Fu[23]	25	Female	University of Tampa	3.6	3L Full-Time	3.5
Gabby[24]	30	Female	Bryant College	3.2	3L Part-Time	3.6
Hugo[25]	27	Male	California State San Bernardino	3.3	3L Full-Time	3.5

After selecting research participants, the next step in my study was to start collecting the data.

---

17. To preserve the anonymity of the students interviewed, each student that participated in this study has been assigned a pseudonym.

18. Interview with Antonio, 3L at Western State College of Law, in Fullerton, Cal. (July 17, 2013).

19. Interview with Bari, 2L at Western State College of Law, in Fullerton, Cal. (July 18, 2013).

20. Interview with Carlota, 3L at Western State College of Law, in Fullerton, Cal. (July 18, 2013).

21. Interview with Denzel, 2L at Western State College of Law, in Fullerton, Cal. (July 18, 2013).

22. Interview with Ester, 3L at Western State College of Law, in Fullerton, Cal. (July 18, 2013).

23. Interview with Fu, 3L at Western State College of Law, in Fullerton, Cal. (July 19, 2013).

24. Interview with Gabby, 3L at Western State College of Law, in Fullerton, Cal. (July 20, 2013).

25. Interview with Hugo, 3L at Western State College of Law, in Fullerton, Cal. (July 20, 2013).

2. Collecting the Study Data

Typically, three kinds of data collection are utilized with qualitative research: interviews, observations, and written documents.[26] For my study, I utilized the interview and written document data collection methods.

To ensure ethical considerations were discussed between myself and the participant, each participant signed an informed consent waiver prior to the interview which acknowledged:

- the study purpose;
- the procedures and benefits of the study;
- the voluntary nature of the study participation;
- the participant's right to stop the study at any time; and
- the procedures used to protect participant confidentiality.

Unstructured, in-depth phenomenological interviews[27] were conducted with students and the questions were directed to their experiences, feelings, beliefs and convictions about the study process they employ before and during the semester. Depending on the participant, interviews lasted approximately three hours, with three of the interviews lasting approximately four hours. It was assumed the participants' responses were accurate to the best of their knowledge.

Some participants brought copies of outlines and condensed outlines to the interview, which were reviewed during and after the interview.[28] I took notes while interviewing participants and only wrote what the participant said at the time of the interview.[29] After the interview, I reviewed my notes, paraphrased some of the testimony and began to interpret some of the data in the margins

---

26. Michael Quinn Patton, M. Q., *Qualitative Evaluation and Research Methods* (2nd ed. 1990).

27. This language was taken from: *A Phenomenological Research Design Illustrated*, Thomas Groenewald, (2004), International Journal of Qualitative Methods, Volume: 3 issue: 1, page(s): 42–55

28. Copies of the documents provided by the participants are maintained in a secure location. Please contact the author if you are interested in reviewing a copy of the documents furnished at the interview.

29. Please contact the author if you are interested in reviewing a copy of the interview notes.

of my notes[30] while being careful not to prematurely categorize or interpret the data or push my bias into the study.

All eight interviews were audio recorded and transcribed verbatim by listening to the recording and simultaneously typing the words spoken during the interviews. Thereafter, each participant signed a confirmation statement that the transcripts were true and correct.

A file was then created for each of the study participants, which included the following information:

- the written informed consent waiver;

- my notes made during the interview;

- my notes made subsequent to the interview;

- all documents the participant offered during the interview;

- any notes made during the data interpretation process;

- the interview transcript;

- the confirmation signed by the participant that the transcript was true and correct; and

- any further communications between myself and the participants.

After collecting data, the next step in my study was to start interpreting the data.

3. Interpreting the Study Data

The qualitative data interpretation design of Thomas Groenewald, articulated in his 2004 article entitled, *A Phenomenological Research Design Illustrated,*[31] was used to interpret my study data. Slight changes were made to Groenewald's terminology for ease of reading in this book. The data interpretation procedure included the following steps:

(a) uncovering the phenomenon;

(b) deciphering the units of meaning and removing redundant units;

---

30. Field notes are a secondary data storage method in qualitative research. Groenewald, *supra* note 93, at 48. Because the human mind tends to forget quickly, field notes by the researcher are crucial in qualitative research to retain data gathered. *Id.*

31. *A Phenomenological Research Design Illustrated,* Thomas Groenewald, (2004), International Journal of Qualitative Methods, Volume: 3 issue: 1, page(s): 42–55.

(c) clustering the remaining units to find "themes";

(d) conducting validity checks with study participants; and

(e) summarizing the general and unique "lived experiences" into a central theme.

a. Uncovering the Phenomenon

I listened to the recorded interviews, taking note of the words of the participants several times over. I reached an understanding of the whole system of beliefs of each of the participants regarding the steps that define their study process.

Table 3 (following four pages) represents the lived experience of the holistic law school study process for each of my study participants.

Table 3: Holistic Law School Study Process

	ANTONIO	BARI	CARLOTA	DENZEL
STEP 1	Find 5 or 6 outlines online and review for big picture of course	Use Lexis Nexis, table of contents and syllabus to create skeleton of large-scale organization of the course	Review chapter titles and sub-titles to understand big picture of course	Read case and translate every paragraph of the opinion into own words; write translation in book margin
STEP 2	Review syllabus to see all topics covered	Read and brief every case in a separate document	Read and brief every case in a separate document; print briefs to bring to class	Brief every case in a separate document and print briefs to bring to class
STEP 3	Using table of contents, fill in topics with information from online outlines	During class, absorb information and interact with discussion	During class, handwrite lecture notes on briefs and handwrite other lecture notes on legal pad	Look at table of contents and create a skeleton outline in a separate document
STEP 4	Read assigned cases holistically	After class, revise outline to conform to professor's lecture	Every 1–3 weeks, synthesize briefs, notes on briefs and lecture notes into an outline; summarize case facts and convert rules into sentences in her own words	During class, take lecture notes (written on briefs) and transfer information from case brief and lecture notes into outline

ESTER	FU	GABY	HUGO
Open table of contents and create skeleton of every chapter	Read and book brief every case	Read and brief cases	Review table of contents, syllabus and cases to determine what the author was "trying to do"
Read cases and book brief or write case briefs; create a separate document for notes taken while reading; print briefs to bring to class	Go to table of contents to see an overall picture of the course and issues covered	Review BARBRI outlines and create skeletal outline based off BARBRI structure	Read cases, ask what he learned from case, rephrase rule in laymen's terms and write the rule for each issue in separate documents
During class, handwrite lecture notes on a legal pad only as to information professor harped on	During class, take lecture notes and incorporate book briefs into lecture notes	During class, take lecture notes directly in the outline	Create hypotheticals and conditionals for every rule: "If A, then B"
After class, combine lecture notes, reading notes and rules from case briefs, that were confirmed in class, into proper category of the skeleton outline	After class, create outline with class notes, rules from cases that are confirmed in class and then write overarching large issue rule	After class, reword lecture notes added to outline to full sentences; color code headings and sub-headings	

continued on next page

Table 3: Holistic Law School Study Process *continued*

	ANTONIO	BARI	CARLOTA	DENZEL
STEP 5	Pull essential rule from case by asking self what the case really was about; narrow rule by determining facts the case was decided upon	Meet with trusted study group and exchange outlines to identify any missed topics that others included; discuss and understand how any missed topics fit within the organization of the course	Review and re-review outline over and over	Get BARBRI outline; verify rules in outline are the same as rules in BARBRI outline; if rules are complete, formulate rules in a manner that will answer an exam question
STEP 6	Check that rule in outline is same as rule pulled from case; if different, understand differences and create new rule	When confident outline is complete, create a condensed outline that changes rules into sentence format and puts in own words	Take practice exams using sentence rules contained in the outline	Take 1–2 practice exams using verified rules and modify rules if they do not flow in the practice exam
STEP 7	During class, confirm rules in outline and understanding of rule are correct	Answer hypotheticals and practice exams using condensed outline	Memorize rules by writing them until committed to memory	Write and re-write all rules until committed to memory
STEP 8	After class, condense outline by revising rules, eliminating redundancy and paraphrasing rules	Write and re-write rules three times to commit to memory		
STEP 9	Memorize condensed outline			

ESTER	FU	GABY	HUGO
Review outline; highlight the headings, sub-headings, relevant notes, cases, definitions and rules	Get together with a friend to create a condensed outline by writing all rules in their outlines in paragraph format (sometimes they create sentences to make the format flow)	Review all case briefs and create a fact trigger that allows her to memorize, apply and distinguish the case; review outline with table of contents to make sure not missing anything	
Assess whether outline flows by writing practice exams; if outline is disjointed, restate rules and condense outline into rules only	Memorize condensed outline by comparing and contrasting the cases and hand-writing the facts and reasoning of every case	Condense outline by shortening rules and her comments on the cases	
Memorize rules by reading or typing them over and over	Review condensed outline and write everything about each of the cases; re-write cases she cannot remember	Review professor sample essay answers and modify condensed outline to look like sample answer	
If professor provides sample answers, break down where the points are most heavily afforded		Memorize condensed outline by saying the outline out loud and taking practice exams	

After exposing the complete law school study process of successful students, the next step in my study was to decipher the important study steps and eliminate redundant study steps.

b. Deciphering the Units of Meaning by Removing Redundant Units

This is a critical phase of interpreting the data because the researcher starts isolating pieces that they believe are important to the phenomenon. This requires the researcher to make substantial judgment calls while consciously bracketing their own presuppositions in order to avoid inappropriate subjective judgments.[32] To do this the researcher considers the literal content and the number of times a meaning was mentioned to determine its significance.

In true phenomenological methodology, I reviewed the factual content contained in each participant's process in Table 3. When I came upon a unit (or study step) that had already been uncovered, I considered the participant's words and my notes taken during the interview, if any, to determine whether the unit was truly redundant or if, despite similar wording, carried a different meaning. If the unit was redundant, I placed a line over the portion that was redundant. If the entire step was redundant, I placed a diagonal line in the redundant unit box.

In doing a cursory review of Table 3, it was easy to decipher main differences and similarities in the eight study processes, creating a starting point for me to remove all of the redundant units.

One main difference was the number of steps each participant employed in their study process during their semester. One participant had a nine-step study process, three participants had an eight-step study process, three participants had a seven-step study process and one participant had a three-step study process. Despite these differences, each study process provided the participant with the same deep understanding of the course material (explained in detail on page 29) and success in the course, notwithstanding that the step may have been completed at a different time or combined with other steps. Why? I couldn't wait to start removing redundant units in Table 3 to provide a comprehensive successful study process where students could pick and choose steps that were essential for their success.

---

32. *See* Groenewald, T. *supra* at footnote 72, p. 19

Even before removing the redundant units, it also started to become clear by looking at Table 3 that several study participants completed similar steps during their individual study process. I physically counted the number of times a word (or word that appeared synonymous with other words) was mentioned collectively in Table 3 to appreciate its significance in the overall study process. Similar skills that started to emerge across Table 3 included: reviewing the table of contents, creating a skeleton outline based on the table of contents, reading cases, briefing cases, reviewing notes taken during the lecture, condensing outlines and committing a condensed outline rules to memory. I could not wait to have a visual of Table 3 without the redundant units: this would be the most comprehensive study process a student could employ to succeed in law school.

Table 4 (following four pages) shows the lines placed through words in the unit that are partially redundant and diagonal lines through entire units that are completely redundant.

Table 4: Deciphering the Units of Meaning by Removing Redundant Units

	ANTONIO	BARI	CARLOTA	DENZEL
STEP 1	Find 5 or 6 outlines online and review for big picture of course	Use Lexis Nexis, table of contents and syllabus to create skeleton of large-scale organization of the course	Review chapter titles and sub-titles ~~to understand big picture of course~~	Read case and translate every paragraph of the opinion into own words; write translation in book margin
STEP 2	~~Review syllabus~~ to see all topics covered	~~Read and brief every case~~ in a separate document	~~Read and brief every case in a separate document;~~ print briefs to bring to class	Brief every case in a separate document and print briefs to bring to class
STEP 3	Using table of contents, fill in topics with information from online outlines	During class, absorb information and interact with discussion	During class, handwrite lecture notes on briefs and handwrite other lecture notes on legal pad	Look at table of contents and create a skeleton outline in a separate document
STEP 4	Read assigned cases holistically	After class, revise outline to conform to professor's lecture	Every 1–3 weeks, synthesize briefs, notes on briefs and lecture notes into an outline; summarize case facts and convert rules into sentences in her own words	During class, take lecture notes (written on briefs) and transfer information from case brief and lecture notes into outline

ESTER	FU	GABY	HUGO
Open table of contents and create skeleton of every chapter	Read and book brief every case	Read and brief cases	~~Review table of contents, sylla-bus and~~ cases to determine what the author was "trying to do"
Read cases and book brief ~~or write case briefs;~~ create a separate document for notes taken while reading; ~~print briefs to bring to class~~	Go to table of contents to see an overall picture of the course and issues covered	Review BARBRI outlines and create skeletal outline based off BARBRI structure	Read cases, ask what he learned from case, rephrase rule in laymen's terms and write the rule for each issue in separate documents
~~During class, hand-write lecture notes on a legal pad~~ only as to information professor harped on	During class, ~~take lecture notes~~ and incorporate book briefs into lecture notes	During class, take lecture notes di-rectly in the outline	Create hypotheti-cals and condition-als for every rule: "If A, then B"
After class, com-bine lecture notes, reading notes and rules from case briefs, that were confirmed in class, into proper catego-ry of the skeleton outline	~~After class, create outline with class notes,~~ rules from cases that are confirmed in class and then write overarching large issue rule	~~After class, reword lecture notes added to outline to full sentences;~~ color code headings and sub-headings	

continued on next page

Table 4: Deciphering the Units of Meaning by Removing Redundant Units *continued*

	ANTONIO	BARI	CARLOTA	DENZEL
STEP 5	Pull essential rule from case by ~~asking self what the case really was about;~~ narrow rule by determining facts the case was decided upon	Meet with trusted study group and exchange outlines to identify any missed topics that others included; discuss and understand how any missed topics fit within the organization of the course	Review and re-review outline over and over	Get BARBRI outline; verify rules in outline are the same as rules in BARBRI outline; if rules are complete, formulate rules in a manner that will answer an exam question
STEP 6	Check that rule in outline is same as rule pulled from case; if different, understand differences and create new rule	When confident outline is complete, ~~create a condensed outline that changes rules into sentence~~ format and puts in own words	Take practice exams using sentence rules contained in the outline	~~Take 1–2 practice exams using verified rules~~ and modify rules if they do not flow in the practice exam
STEP 7	During class, confirm rules in outline and understanding of rule are correct	Answer hypotheticals and ~~practice exams~~ using condensed outline	Memorize rules by writing them until committed to memory	Write and re-write all rules until committed to memory
STEP 8	~~After class, condense outline by revising rules,~~ eliminating redundancy and paraphrasing rules	~~Write and re-write rules three times to commit to memory~~		
STEP 9	Memorize condensed outline			

ESTER	FU	GABY	HUGO
~~Review outline~~; highlight the headings, sub-headings, relevant notes, cases, definitions and rules	Get together with a friend to create a condensed outline by writing all rules in their outlines in paragraph format (sometimes they create sentences to make the format flow)	Review all case briefs and create a fact trigger that allows her to memorize, apply and distinguish the case; review outline with table of contents to make sure not missing anything	
Assess whether outline flows by writing practice exams; if outline is disjointed, restate rules and condense outline into rules only	Memorize condensed outline by comparing and contrasting the cases and handwriting the facts and reasoning of every case	Condense outline by shortening rules and her comments on the cases	
Memorize rules by reading or typing them over and over	Review condensed outline and write everything about each of the cases; re-write cases she cannot remember	Review professor sample essay answers and modify condensed outline to look like sample answer	
If professor provides sample answers, break down where the points are most heavily afforded		Memorize condensed outline by saying the outline out loud and taking practice exams	

Thereafter, I was left with the most comprehensive picture of what successful law students did when they studied. I took those units that were not crossed out of Table 3 and placed them into one paragraph as follows:

Prior to the course starting, successful students review one or more of the following to gain a big picture/large-scale organization of the course and to see all of the topics covered in the course: 5–6 course outlines found online, a Lexis Nexis course outline, the table of contents, the syllabus and textbook chapter titles and sub-titles. Successful students read cases holistically and brief or book brief every case, determine what the author was trying to do by including the case in the text, translate every paragraph of the opinion into their own words and write their translation in the margin of the textbook, ask themselves what they learned from the case, rephrase the rule they learned in laymen's terms, write their own rule for every major issue covered, create their own hypotheticals from facts in the opinion, apply those hypotheticals to the rule in the case, create conditionals for every rule (i.e., if "A" then "B") and narrow the rule by determining which facts the case was decided upon. Successful law students create a separate document for notes taken while reading their cases and print their case briefs and bring hardcopies of the case briefs to class. Successful law students create skeletal outlines based off BARBRI outlines. During class, successful students absorb information, interact with the discussions, handwrite lecture notes on the hard copy of their case briefs, handwrite lecture notes or information the professor harped on in class on a separate legal pad, incorporate book briefs into lecture notes, take lecture notes directly in their outline, confirm rules in outline and understanding of rule are correct and transfer information from their lecture notes and case briefs into their outlines. After class, successful students either create an outline with rules they re-wrote but which were also confirmed in class or revise their existing outlines to conform to the class lecture. After class, successful students synthesize briefs, notes on briefs and lecture notes into an outline, summarize case facts and convert rules into sentences in their own words and highlight the headings, sub-headings, relevant notes, cases, definitions and rules. Successful students either (1) meet with a trusted study group to exchange outlines, identify missed issues that others might have included and discuss and understand how missed issues fit within the organization of the course or (2) get a BARBRI outline and cross-verify that the rules contained in their outline are the same as rules in BARBRI outline — if rules are complete, they reformulate the rules in a manner that will answer an exam question or (3) they get together with a friend to create a condensed outline by writing all rules in their outlines in paragraph format, sometimes creating sentences to make the format flow or (4) verify that rule in their outline is the same as the rule pulled from the case — if different, they try to understand differences and create new rule or (5) Review all case briefs and create a fact trigger that allows the student to memorize, apply and distinguish the case or (6) review outline with table of contents to make sure the outline is not missing anything. When the successful student is confident the outline is complete, they eliminate redundancies, continue to paraphrase rules, take practice exams using sentence rules contained in the outline, assess whether the outline flows by writing practice exams, restate rules if outline is disjointed and condense outline into rules only. Before the exam, the successful student reviews the condensed outline, writes everything about each of the cases, re-writes cases they cannot remember, reviews professor sample essay answers and modifies the condensed outline to look like sample answer, or, if the professor provides sample answers, the student breaks down where the points are most heavily afforded. Immediately before the exam, the successful student memorizes rules by writing them until committed to memory, by reading or typing them over and over and by repeating them out loud.

While the aforementioned paragraph is dense, for the first time, the comprehensive phenomenon of what successful students do to study in law school started to unfold.

After deciphering true units and eliminating redundant units, the next step in my study was look at the data remaining in Table 4 and identify any themes to expose the essence of the successful study process.

c. Clustering the Remaining Units to Find the Central Theme

In this step, clusters of themes are typically formed by grouping units of meaning together and identifying significant topics.[33] It is important for the researcher to go back to the recorded interview and to the list of non-redun-

---

33. *Id.*

dant units of meaning to derive clusters of appropriate meaning.[34] Often there is overlap in the clusters, which can be expected, considering the nature of human phenomena.[35] By interrogating the meaning of the various clusters central themes are determined, which expresses the essence of these clusters.[36]

Among many others, the following questions were considered while reviewing the units in Table 2 and Table 3 to identify themes:

- Did student learning preferences impact the different study process?
- Why did every student have steps in their process?
- Did the study process emerge as a result of other unsuccessful study attempts?
- Why were these students better at assessing their own study strengths and weaknesses?
- What do each of these different humans do that is similar when studying?
- Are there any common threads, other than the actual study step, that these students do when studying?
- Why do some successful students have more or fewer steps than others?
- How do these students know how to do these steps?
- Why are successful students completing these steps?
- What motivates these successful students?
- Is it possible for me to understand their motivation and give that same motivation to other students?
- Do successful students have a different mindset that makes them move from step to step without stopping?

After hours of reviewing the interview transcripts and tables, the central theme emerged clearly. Armed for the first time with a central theme that I believed to uncover the phenomenon of the successful study process, I eagerly conducted the next two steps to complete my study.

---

34. *Id.*
35. *Id.*
36. *Id.*

d. Conducting Validity Checks with Study Participants

When the central theme is uncovered, the researcher conducts a "validity check" by returning to the study participants to determine if the essence of the interview has been correctly captured in the researcher's central theme, and any modification necessary is done as result of this "validity check."[37]

In true phenomenological methodology, I conducted validity checks with the eight study participants and made only minor changes.

e. Summarizing the Unique Lived Experiences into a Central Theme

The phenomenon (of what a successful law student does to succeed in law school) was confirmed by my research participants.

The central theme that emerged after considering all of the data in the clustering stage is that every law student had a very specific step-by-step study process *and* every step of the study process was motivated by two clear goals: (1) to understand course material, and (2) to succeed in the course.

The central theme of the study process was further interpreted into ten categories below, which represent the most important information interpreted in my study.

i. Successful Law Students Are Motivated by an Internal Reward System That Fuels Them to Continue Studying

The "means" in the study process are the steps undertaken by the students during the study process, and the "ends" happen when the student gains an understanding of course materials and succeeds in the course. The ends — the understanding and success — function much like a trophy, rewarding the successful law student for the mental warfare they have put themselves through *while completing each step in the study process.*

Successful students vehemently strive for the "rewards" they gain upon completion of each step in their study process. The reward then motivates the student to complete the next step. In a way, the reward makes the student feel competent and thus ready to tackle the next step in the process, and the motivation reignites at the commencement of the next step. The means and ends build confidence in successful students, making them ready to attack any sub-

---

37. *Id.*

ject because they are equipped with a winning strategy that not only makes them happy but also produces results.

ii. Successful Law Students Take Intentional Steps When Studying

Each step in the successful students' process was intentionally executed for a specific purpose. By being intentional, the successful student is aware of what they want to achieve, and they are purposeful in every study step, which is meaningful and fulfilling to students. Being intentional also allows a student to feel a high level of autonomy because they are making their own decisions about studying and prioritizing tasks in their schedule. Last, being intentional about their study process forces the student to question the value of each step and whether they truly receive the reward (discussed above) they get from completing each step.

iii. Successful Law Students Can Articulate the Various Steps They Take and Explain Why They Do Them

Successful students are acutely aware of and can express their study steps and the reasons they do them. Being able to articulate their steps and basis for doing them is important because it has an impact on how their professors and other students receive their conversations in class, office hours and study groups. If others can clearly understand the student, they can give appropriate feedback. There is less of a breakdown in communication, which leads to less confusion and saves precious time overall. Being able to articulate their process also makes the student appear more knowledgeable in class and confident in front of their professors, without having to stumble over their words. They have carefully thought about the material and are not winging it. Last, being able to articulate their process makes successful students aware of their law school strengths and weaknesses so they continuously better themselves.

iv. Successful Law Students View Studying as a Personal (Sometimes Fun) Challenge

Have you ever heard a successful law student say that "law school is fun"? Before reading this book, you may have rolled your eyes upon hearing that statement. However, now you can see why this statement is true for successful law students. They aren't being arrogant. They are being honest. The reason successful students don't always view studying as drudgery is because they view each step in the study process as a challenge, which is in line with law students' (healthy) competitive nature. Successful law students overcome the challenge when they gain understanding, which only comes from completing each step in the study process. Successful law students see this as a small victory. Thus, studying is a constant, cyclical internal "game" for successful students to engage in, which they think is, well, *fun*. Successful students are relentless until they "win" the law school competition in their minds, and that is why they view the law school experience as a pleasurable one.

v. Successful Law Students Put in the Time to Study but Spend Less Time Studying than Other Students (Not Because They Are Smarter but Because They Do the Steps So Often That They Master Steps and Can Thus Accomplish Them Quicker)

Remember, successful law students are not smarter than other law students who perform less than what they know they are capable of. Successful law students don't just automatically grasp content. Instead, they know that understanding material does not happen overnight. They patiently go through their study process with every topic in the course, careful not to rush and cognizant of the time it will take them to realistically complete their study steps. Knowing this, the successful student does not skip a step in their study process. This guarantees their success. Ultimately, the successful student completes the steps in their study process so many times that they become an expert in completing each step in their study process. Mastering how to do the step leads to the successful student executing the step quicker. The repetitive nature of the process develops a sense of automaticity with the process.

Grit elevates the intellect. Every time.

vi. Successful Law Students Realize That the Study Process Is Applicable to and Should Be Done for Every Subject

Successful students do not waste time reinventing the (study process) wheel with every new subject. Instead, they view the study process as a portable skill that they complete for every subject. They know that if they do the steps in every course, they *will* understand their course material and ultimately succeed in the course.

vii. Successful Law Students Have Lower Stress Levels, Which Allows More Brain Power to Be Spent on Understanding Course Material

Juxtapose the successful law student mentality with that of a student who does not have a law school study process in place. Not having a process to follow means the student is completing study tasks like reading, briefing and attending classes without a clear purpose. Instead, these students are aimlessly (but oftentimes fervently) completing random study tasks, which appear in their exam preparation materials as an unorganized, brain-barf of information. A lack of purpose and a lack of understanding compound with the stress the disorganized feeling commonly brings on.

All of this leads to a lack of motivation to achieve the goals which they are often unaware exist. It's almost as if these students do not want to go anywhere near the tangled web of information they have compiled in their courses — it's tantamount to looking at a large pile of laundry (that you loathe doing) that gets bigger every day with each outfit you wear, smellier with added workout gear and which leaves you feeling like you can never catch up (for the record, this is a pure example I've never experienced in my life,[38] but you get the point of how stinky stuff snowballs?).

Like dominoes, since there is no study process in play, there is no passion to push oneself to the next step, and oftentimes, unsuccessful students don't complete all of the steps necessary to succeed in law school. This student, despite studying crazy hours (or perhaps studying not enough hours), despite insane intelligence, despite first-rate entering credentials that would suggest they should succeed in law school — will report after a failed exam that they thought they knew the law but, for some reason, could not explain their understanding on the actual exam.

When there is no understanding of the course material it will always lead to a lack of success in the course. Each of these setbacks lead to confusion, which ends in a lack of confidence and much stress. Did I mention stress? Have you ever heard an unsuccessful student say, "I feel like I am in a hole I can't get out of"? Or how about, "law school is suffocating me"? Now you can see why — the dirty laundry has broken the basket.

Successful students do not go down this anxiety-ridden rabbit hole. Therefore, they aren't experiencing stress every week of the semester, which allows them to sleep better, have more patience and maintain a better work-ethic.

---

38. Just please don't ask my dad!

They aren't distracted easily because they enthusiastically want to win the study challenge that they've set for themselves. They actually have time to see family and friends, which makes them feel normal and happy.

viii. The Motivation to Study in Law School Comes from Fellow Students, Not Professors or Other Influencers

This is not a dig against law school professors and other important people who the law student relies upon for support, guidance and instruction.[39] And of course there are exceptions. However, my study participants emphatically expressed that no one could better understand what they go through in law school than their classmates. Hearing a fellow student give study advice or offer a shoulder to lean on was more meaningful to the successful student in the moment because it felt more genuine coming from someone entrenched in law school. Fellow classmates motivate students in a way that others cannot.

I've sat through many meetings and conferences across the country pondering how to motivate students to do the work to make them succeed in law school. Those conversations often end in an all too familiar, "you can lead a horse to water, but you can't make it drink ..." conclusion. That belief has never resonated well with me (an exceedingly passionate academic support professor). When professors give students detailed goals and tell them how to achieve them, why were students still failing to achieve them? What are we missing here?

I was having a conversation with my older brother Anthony, a highly successful and brilliant IT business owner, about the results of my qualitative study. He said that he was interested in doing a similar qualitative study about the phenomenon that makes his own employees successful in their jobs. Anthony wanted to then use the data from his study to teach future employees that if they did the process uncovered in his study, they would achieve the overall goals *Anthony had in mind for his business.*

In that moment, I realized how the data from my qualitative study could clear the fog on how to motivate law students to do the work. Law professors

---

39. If you know me, you wouldn't question the level of respect I share for my colleagues who spend unquantifiable amounts of time supporting and teaching our law students or the family members and friends of the law students who support them unconditionally. But this central theme was repeated enough times throughout the study such that it was uncovered as a central theme.

create course goals and learning objectives to assess the effectiveness of *their* teaching during the semester. Similarly, law professors create detailed grading rubrics to assess how students perform on the exams *they* created. Law professors even sometimes provide students with the structure of the how *they* want the law written on an exam. Law professors give students everything they need to succeed. However, despite these exceptional efforts form their professors, some students still receive low grades in their courses.

The reason for this is that the aforementioned targets and rubrics are personal goals of the professor. They are not the goals of current students, knee deep in the law. Teaching goals are distinct from ends that motivate a student to move from step to step in the study process.

As an analogy, have you ever wondered why a kid is more likely to do something (that you may have tried to get them to do a hundred times) when they are with their friends? I can tell my five-year-old son to eat his broccoli. I can give him a bowl, fill it with perfectly seasoned broccoli and place it in front of him. I know that if he eats the broccoli, he will receive what I believe to be health benefits. However, unless my son adopts the health benefit as his own purpose for eating broccoli, he won't be motivated to eat the broccoli because there is no genuine goal attached to it. When I attend his classroom preschool party and he is sitting in those cute little chairs with his other pint-sized buddies, he eats broccoli with no thought. This is because he sees other peers eating it, and he does what the others are doing. Perhaps he wants to be included, maybe he doesn't want to be different. Maybe he isn't thinking about it at all. But he hears his buddies select broccoli as their side and without skipping a beat, he does the same. He eats broccoli, not because of my health goals associated with eating the broccoli, but because of the goals that are personal to him, in that moment. These motivators come from him, when he is happy doing what he wants, and they are also persuaded by the peers around him.

According to my study participants, motivating a student to move from skill to skill in the study process similarly has little to do with a professor's goals for the course (other than the fact that both the professor wants to teach and the student wants to learn the same topics). Motivation to jump from step to step in the study process is not a stimulus that a professor can give a student because the incentive to move from step to step while studying is fueled by the student *who is actually going through the law school study process*. Law students are internally motivated to study (or figuratively, eat their broccoli) by knowing and feeling that they genuinely gain something from each step in their study process. The "something" they gain is the understanding that each step brings — not meeting a professor's goal. My qualitative study uncovered that the understanding has to come from the student's own experience or the experience of another student deeply engaged in the study process.

As such, I went back to my study data and uncovered the students' own words about what motivated them to execute each step of their study process. The motivation is organized into two categories for each step: (1) how each step leads to an understanding of the course material, and (2) how each step leads to success in the course. If we give future students motivation from their peers to complete each step in the study process, they too will be motivated to do the work to succeed in law school.

With the last five paragraphs happening in my brain during my conversation with my brother Anthony, I simultaneously replied, "Your employees will never be motivated to succeed in your company if the goals for success are created by you. Instead, the goal — *the reason motivating your employees to complete each step in the successful business process, to make them successful employees* — has to come directly from them. After asking your employees to articulate each step, ask your employees why each step in their process makes them successful. *Their response* to that question is what will *motivate* your *future employees* to be successful as well."

ix. Qualitative Research Is for Anyone Who Wants
     to Uncover a Phenomenon

What makes for a successful relationship? What makes people perceive politicians in a positive or negative light? How do I get the accountants in my firm to increase customer service reviews? How do we motivate children to do their chores? What is the meaning of true happiness? How do experts (in anything) become experts? How do I achieve my dreams? All of these phenomena can be answered by conducting a qualitative phenomenological study to uncover the lived experiences of others who have placed meaning in these occurrences.

This chapter provides the template for doing just that. The opportunities are endless. See also Appendix A, "Quick Template for Conducting Qualitative Phenomenological Research."

x. Successful Law Students Incorporate Their Study
Process into a Weekly Schedule

The best way to relieve stress is to make a list of tasks you have to complete, prioritize them and accomplish them. Just knowing what you have to do eliminates anxiety. Successful law students place their study steps into weekly chunks because their professors give them assignments to complete on a weekly basis. Chapter 3 explains how to incorporate *Nine Steps* for each subject into a weekly calendar.

Conclusion

For the first time there exists a scientifically proven, successful, step-by-step law school study process that provides the motivation for law students to do the work. Armed with this book, professors now have a common language to motivate students, and all law students can and will succeed if they follow this process.

Aren't you dying to read the process in Chapter 2 so you too can start having fun in law school? Read the next page!

CHAPTER TWO

The Nine-Step Study Process for Success in Law School

Have you ever driven to work and after a few minutes of thinking about something during the drive, notice you're already halfway there but don't necessarily remember the entire drive? Have you ever been driving to one place but accidentally got off the freeway on the exit you used to take to get to your old apartment? This is because you have traveled these routes hundreds, if not thousands, of times in your life. The driving patterns become automatic and monotonous as your brain commits them to memory and adopts them as routine episodes of your day.

Despite that you may have studied before, studying in law school is not as intuitive. For many novice law students, it's unlike any other experience they've had in their life, academic or otherwise. Therefore, students cannot simply go to law school and, in addition to feeling the normal pressures of the intense new environment, automatically employ a successful study process (or even be aware that one exists).

To be successful in law school, students must perform a multitude of skills that happen before the course begins and throughout the semester. Some skills are performed chronologically, and other skills are executed simultaneously.

In chronological order and in short form, here is the nine-step, scientifically proven, successful law student study process:

Step 1: Gain Big-Picture Understanding of the Subject

Step 2: Create a Skeleton Outline for Each Main Topic in the Course

Step 3: Actively Read Every Case You Are Assigned

Step 4: Brief Every Case You Are Assigned in Your Topic Outline

Step 5: Print the Relevant Portion of Your Outline and Bring It to Class

Step 6: In Class, Confirm Your Understanding of What You Taught Yourself

Step 7: Transform the Outline into a Topic Approach

Step 8: Write Practice Essays Using Your Topic Approach

Step 9: Get Feedback from Your Professor and Study Group and Solidify Your Topic Approach

For each of the nine steps, you will learn: (1) how to do the step by completing a skill; (2) how that skill will help you understand course material; and (3) how completing that skill will equate to success in the course.

The Nine-Step Law School Study Process Was Created by Your Law Student Peers, Not Your Professors

It is important to remember that I did not create the nine-step successful study process — it came from the successful law students in my study. In true qualitative fashion, the language used by the successful student participants, as they explained their study process during the interview phase of the study, has not been changed. If the law school study process that emerged from my study data had been tampered with (to sound more "professor-ish" or to make a scholarly point) the entire qualitative study would have been compromised and thus of no use to you or me. So, if your law professor disagrees with the process (which would be surprising) or your study group studies differently, that is okay. Perhaps try to assess why but rest assured that the nine-step study process is the process *your successful peers* are implementing to succeed in law school.

Eight Short Tips on How to Employ the Nine-Step Successful Law School Study Process

First, you have properly completed each study step when you achieve the understanding of material and success brought about by completing the step. As explained in Chapter 1, these achievements are your rewards for doing the hard work, which in turn will motivate you to tackle the next step. It's a cyclical personal challenge for you to dominate.

Second, a few of the steps contain options on how to complete the step — this is because not every successful student in the qualitative study performed the skill in the same manner. While the goals (completing the skill, understanding the material and succeeding in the course) were similar across the board in the study, the manner in which different students tackled the skill was not always the same. Thus, for a few steps, you will be given to options and can select which one works best for your learning preferences.

Third, whenever you hit a snag in your studying, it can be helpful to reference the specific step where the confusion started. Did you fully identify each topic you were supposed to learn, as listed in your syllabus? If not, re-do Step 2 and fully identify each topic covered in your syllabus. Did you misunderstand a case in class or pull an incorrect rule? If so, check Steps 3, 4 and 7. When you take the time to articulate the source of your substantive misunderstanding, you can quickly see which step in the study process is the culprit of your confusion.

Fourth, this process should be employed in every class. Meaning, you should complete Steps 1 through 9 for every substantive course you take in law school. While I recommend new or struggling students complete all nine steps, you may not need to complete every step, depending on your law school skill level. Likewise, you may find you are already doing some of the steps — try to add in the other steps that are not currently in your study process and assess whether your grades increase as a result. I am confident they will.

Fifth, for most of the steps, you will see a short paragraph entitled, "Lisa's Quick Tips."[1] These are my quick opinions, based on my own experience and expertise with the successful study process, and are intended to supplement the study participants' actual words.

Sixth, remember that this book tells you how to complete the successful law school study process. It is not intended to provide a detailed analysis of the meaning of every skill in the process — these are two different things. It is assumed that you have a very basic knowledge of law school skills. I was intentionally careful not to write a lengthy book defining various law school skills because that takes away from the simplicity of the study process. I've incorporated as much of a definition for every skill that I feel necessary for you to complete the study process, however, if you read a step and are still unsure how

---

1. This term was coined by my brilliant nine-year-old, William A. Blasser, VI (and yes, he asked me to include his middle initial).

to execute it (i.e., how to brief a case, for example) there is an ocean of books out there that can define that skill for you.

Seventh, for a quick reference on the study steps without any explanations, see Appendix B: Successful Study Process Quick Reference Table.

Eighth, for a quick reference on the study steps with explanations see Appendix C: Successful Study Process with Explanations Quick Reference Table.

Ready? Set. Go!

STEP 1: BEFORE THE SEMESTER STARTS

Gain a Big-Picture Understanding of the Subject

1. Successful Law Students Do This Skill:

Find and read subject-specific commercial outlines, outlines from other students who took the course with the same professor or outlines from students who took the course with a different professor.

2. Successful Law Students' Explanation of How This Skill Leads to an Understanding of Course Material

This skill provides you with a big picture of all of the main topics and sub-topics covered in a course so you can visualize the relationships (or lack thereof) between the topics and sub-topics and understand the totality of what you might learn when the semester begins.

3. Successful Law Students' Explanation of How This Skill Equates to Success in the Course

This step provides you with an all-inclusive framework of the subject without the pressure of having to understand every intricate piece. It makes every subsequent step in the study process easier because you will have already reviewed the topics in the subject once and each new topic won't appear as daunting on its second read. It's comforting to read something you already know about.

4. Lisa's Quick Tip

A commercial outline is one written by a company specializing in law school and bar preparation study aides and is typically not associated with a law school. There are so many commercial outlines available to law students from so many different sources. Contact your Academic Support Department to see if they can recommend a specific commercial outline that your professor prefers.[2] Oftentimes other successful law students are willing to share their outlines if you ask them, but reassure them that your purpose in reviewing their outline is not to copy their work. Also, a simple Google search will yield other law students outlines on subjects you are currently taking—it does not matter that the outline comes from another school because your sole purpose in reviewing the outline is to gain a big picture of what the subject entails, not learn the intricacies of the material.

Furthermore, first-year courses typically last two semesters (i.e., Torts I and Torts II). So, if you review a commercial outline that covers the entire subject before taking Torts I, be mindful that you may not be learning everything that you review in the commercial outline in Torts I. Despite this, the study participants still reported this as the first step in their study process.

STEP 2: BEFORE CLASS

Create a Skeleton Outline for Each Main Topic in the Course

1. Successful Law Students Do This Skill:

Open your syllabus and review the reading the professor has assigned for the semester, paying close attention to how the professor organized the topics and sub-topics.

---

2. You can also email me with any of these sorts of questions, anytime. My email is lblasser@blasserlaw.com and I would love to be a source of reference for you.

Next, write down a list of the main topics (as written in the syllabus) you are responsible for learning all semester.

Next, open your textbook table of contents and view the table of contents for the pages assigned in the syllabus.

Then, open a Word document and create a skeleton outline that mirrors the table of contents for the pages you are assigned to read. Create one outline for each main topic that includes the headings, sub-headings and case names as they are listed and appear in the table of contents.

2. Successful Law Students' Explanation of How This Skill Leads to an Understanding of Course Material

This skill provides a detailed frame of main topics and sub-topics that your professor expects you to master. It also allows you to categorize topics and place very specific information that you must learn within each topic. Although this step requires no substantive knowledge, it provides confidence at the beginning of the semester because you have touched and organized each of the main topics and sub-topics before the semester begins. You are then aware of exactly how many issues you will learn, which makes the course feel more "doable."

3. Successful Law Students' Explanation of How This Skill Equates to Success in the Course

If you grasp from the outset that there are main topics which are comprised of several sub-topics, you are more likely to (1) separate the main issues when you write a midterm or final exam, (2) understand which parts of the sub-issues are relevant and irrelevant to the fact pattern (saving time to focus analysis on the proper issues during the exam), (3) follow IRAC for each topic and its sub-topics, and (4) apply the correct facts to the correct topic/sub-topic.

4. Example

Table 5 is an excerpt (week 1 through 5) of a sample assignment chart contained in a Torts I syllabus.[3]

---

3. This assignment chart was taken, with permission, from the assignment chart in the Torts I syllabus of Professor Susan Keller, a dear colleague and professor of law at Western State College of Law in Irvine, California.

Table 5: Excerpt from a Sample Syllabus Assignment Chart

Week	Topic	Assignment	Cases
1	Introduction to Tort Law Introduction to Intent	1–46 685–688, 695–706	*White v. Muniz* (695) *Villa v. Derouen* (697) *Doe v. Johnson* (704)
2	Battery & Assault Applying and Distinguishing Cases	Case Handout 1 707–715	*McCracken v. Sloan* (handout) *Leichtman v. WLW Jacor* (707)
3	Intentional Infliction of Emotional Distress False Imprisonment	715–748	*Brandon v. City of* *Richardson* (716) *Alcorn v. Anbro* (727) *Swenson v. Northern* *Crop Ins.* (729) *Graham v. Guilderland* *Cent. Sch. Dist.* (731) *Wal-Mart Stores v.* *Cockrell* (741)
4	Other Intentional Torts: Trespass Trespass to Chattels Conversion Privileges: Consent	Restatement 2d, Handout 798–802 749–757 Consent Handout 757–767	*Creel v. Crim* (798) *U.S. v. Arora* (749) *Hogan v. Tavzel* (757) *Hellriegel v. Tholl* (759) *Reavis v. Slominski* (761)
5	Privileges: Self-Defense Necessity	768–777 781–784, 787 n. 7	*Bradley v. Hunter* (768) *Juarez-Martinez v.* *Deans* (770) *Rossi v. Del Luca* (781) *Vincent v. Lake Erie* (782)

From the assignment chart in the syllabus, the student is able to visualize and write down a list of topics they should expect to learn in torts (for week 1 through 5, in this example), which would look like Table 6:

Table 6: Sample List of Topics from Syllabus

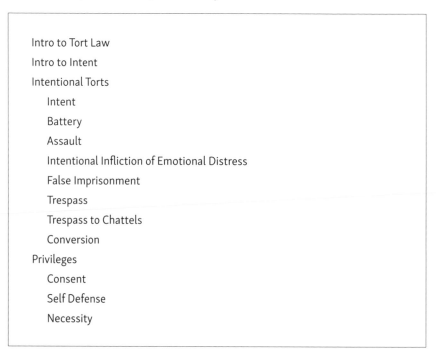

Intro to Tort Law

Intro to Intent

Intentional Torts

  Intent

  Battery

  Assault

  Intentional Infliction of Emotional Distress

  False Imprisonment

  Trespass

  Trespass to Chattels

  Conversion

Privileges

  Consent

  Self Defense

  Necessity

The list of topics in Table 6 is a checklist of what you need to learn for the final. For the first week of class, the student was assigned to read pages 1–46, 685–688 and 695–706. Assume Table 7 is a table of contents for pages 1–46:[4]

---

4. Modified from the table of contents in *Tort Law & Practice* (5th ed.), Vetri, Levine, Vogel and Gassama, Carolina Academic Press.

Table 7: Sample Table of Contents Covering First Topic in Torts

The table of contents tells the student everything they need to know for the first topic covered in Week 1: Introduction to Tort Law. From the table of contents, the student would then create one outline for each topic. The skeletal outline the student would create for first topic (Intro to Tort Law) assigned for Week 1 on pages 1–46, would start to look like Table 8:

Table 8: Sample Skeletal Outline Covering First Topic in Torts

I. Intro to Torts
  A. History of Accidents
  B. History of Tort Law in America
II. Culpability for Torts
  A. Intended Harm: Intentional Torts:
    1. *Gonzalez v. Smith:*
      FACTS:
      PROC. HISTORY:
      RULE/REASONING:
      MY THOUGHTS:
  B. Unintended Harm:
    1. *Jamison v. Mad*
      FACTS:
      PROC. HISTORY:
      RULE/REASONING:
      MY THOUGHTS:

You do not need to do any reading to organize your skeletal outline. You are merely doing a skill to set yourself up to learn the topic. Assume that the table of contents for the remaining reading assigned in Week 1, pages 685–688 and 696–706,[5] looks like Table 9:

Table 9: Sample Table of Contents Covering Second Topic in Torts

---

5. *Id.*

The skeletal outline the student would create for pages 685–688 and 696–706 would look like Table 10:

Table 10: Sample Skeletal Outline Covering Second Topic in Torts

I. Intentional Torts

  A. Assault, Battery and Intentional Infliction of Emotional Distress

    1. *Dickens v. Puryear*

    FACTS:

    PROC. HISTORY:

    RULE/REASONING:

    MY THOUGHTS:

  B. Meaning of Intent

    1. *White v. Muniz*

    FACTS:

    PROC. HISTORY:

    RULE/REASONING:

    MY THOUGHTS:

    2. *Villa v. Derouen*

    FACTS:

    PROC. HISTORY:

    RULE/REASONING:

    MY THOUGHTS:

    3. *Doe. v. Johnson*

    FACTS:

    PROC. HISTORY:

    RULE/REASONING:

    MY THOUGHTS:

The assignment chart in the syllabus tells the students what topics they will cover each week. By completing Step 2, students can easily see that they will learn two topics in their first week of torts: an introduction to torts and an introduction to intent. Every time the student learns a new topic, the student needs to create a new skeletal outline for that topic.

5. Lisa's Quick Tip

Create one folder on your computer desktop for each subject. Save all of the skeletal outlines from one course in the appropriate subject folder. At the end of the semester, you should have one outline for each main topic you learned in the course. In the Step 2 example, the students' Torts folder on their desktop should contain four outlines because, according to the assignment chart, the student covered four topics during weeks 1 through 5: (1) Intro to Torts, (2) Intent in Torts, (3) Intentional Torts, and (4) Privileges.

Creating skeletal outlines sets you up for future steps. You will fill these skeletal outlines in when you read cases and supplements, brief your cases and attend class, all of which happen in subsequent steps in the successful study process.

STEP 3: BEFORE CLASS

Actively Read Every Case That You Are Assigned

1. Successful Law Students Do This Skill:

Read every case assigned in the syllabus each week, every week. Don't fall behind the syllabus. For every paragraph of the decision, translate what occurred in your own words and/or with drawings. Write your translations in the margin of your textbook.

2. Successful Law Students' Explanation of How This Skill Leads to an Understanding of Course Material

This step requires you to monitor your own understanding of the material.[6] It forces you to be present and focused while reading difficult material. If you cannot translate the material into your own words, that is a cue that you *do not understand the material* and must then determine what needs to be done — in that exact moment — to ensure you meet the goal of understanding the legal issue raised in the case.

3. Successful Law Students' Explanation of How This Skill Equates to Success in the Course

If you understand what you are reading in the moment, you will be more engaged in class because you won't be confused and can instead follow along. You will be excited for the professor to call on you in class so you can showcase what you taught yourself. Monitoring your knowledge allows you to spend far less time memorizing immediately before a midterm or final, leaving ample time for more critical writing practice before the midterm or final.

4. Lisa's Quick Tip

Active reading in law school means that you understand the legal significance of every paragraph in your case opinions. If you do not understand the material when you are reading it there are several things you can do in that moment to gain clarification. First, figure out what specifically is confusing you (is it the entire subject, a topic or sub-topic) and then read a supplement on that particular subject, topic or sub-topic to see if it helps you understand the case. See if your professor recommends any supplements in her or his syllabus and start there. Otherwise, look at the commercial outline you purchased for Step 1. Or, call a trusted study partner for help or schedule a meeting with your professor to discuss the confusion. You can also pull up an online legal research engine, enter the case citation and read a summary of the case, which is typically written in

---

6. This is a term used by Ruth A. McKinney in her book, *Reading Like a Lawyer*, which I have used for over a decade in my Introduction to Legal Methods course. This term coincidentally came out of the mouths of the study participants when they were explaining how Step 3 lead to an understanding of course material.

easy-to-understand language. If you do look at an online source, be cognizant that the case may be heavily edited in your textbook but not in the online version.

STEP 4: BEFORE CLASS

Brief Every Case You Are Assigned and Place It in Your Topic Outline

1. Successful Law Students Do This Skill:

Pick one of the following options:

Option 1: Brief every case you read directly in your skeletal outline. Ask yourself why the author of your textbook included the case in the chapter under the heading/sub-heading it falls under in the table of contents. Narrow the rule by determining which facts, policy or circumstance the case was decided upon. Re-write the rule of each case in your own words.

Option 2: Brief every case and place the brief into a document separate from your skeletal outline. Ask yourself why the author of your textbook included the case in the chapter under the heading/sub-heading within which it falls. Narrow the rule by determining which facts, policy or circumstance the case was decided upon. Re-write the rule of each case in your own words.

Option 3: Book brief every case you read. Narrow the rule by determining which facts, policy or circumstance the case was decided upon. Re-write the rule of each case in your own words.

2. Successful Law Students' Explanation of How This Skill Leads to an Understanding of Course Material

Briefing forces you to distill the most important parts of the case. Placing the brief into your topic outline allows you to visualize the topics and sub-topics that the author of the textbook thought required a case to illuminate a particular issue or an interesting factual scenario. You can also see where the points will be on the exam because if there are seven cases on one topic but only one on another, that's a hint that the topic with more cases is important. Narrowing the rule forces you to boil the case down to the specific fact(s) the case was decided upon. Doing so allows you to see which facts are integral to the decision and which facts your professor might "play with" in terms of testing whether the case would have the same outcome should different facts apply.

3. Successful Law Students' Explanation of How This Skill Equates to Success in the Course

Briefing cases while outlining and reading simultaneously forces you to cover and prepare everything in one place, at one time. The topic outlines contain every piece of information the student needs to know (minus Step 6) for each topic and all of its sub-topics on the midterm and final exam. This is important because when it comes time to transform the outlines in Step 7 (the most important step), you will not waste time flipping through several documents (that do not follow the table of contents or syllabus), in an effort to synthesize the materials. Reading, briefing and outlining every week as you read saves time for critical thinking in class and saves coveted time before midterms and finals to practice writing.

4. Lisa's Quick Tip

A case brief is a written summary of the main points of a case. It generally includes the following components: case name, parties, procedural history, facts, issue, rule, reasoning and outcome. See Table 10 for an example of how a case brief looks in a topic outline. Some professors have specific briefing requirements and collect case briefs while others do not. Typically, the case brief is not a graded assignment and is sufficient if it helps you remember the most important pieces of the case in class.

The difference between Option 1 and Options 2 and 3 is that you are briefing cases directly in your topic outline versus placing them in a separate document or in your book. If you are a new law student, it is strongly recommended that you employ Option 1 because if you brief cases in your topic outline, all of the information you learned on that topic will be in one place—you won't spend time trying to synthesize a separate document full of running briefs or words in your book margins back into your topic outline. Save yourself time!

Also, some students worry that the outline will be too lengthy if they brief directly in their outline. However, remember that each topic gets its own outline, making the length of the topic outline manageable. Again, see Table 10.

Steps 3 (reading the assigned reading) and 4 (briefing the cases as you read them) should happen simultaneously. Reading the professor's assigned reading, briefing cases directly in your topic outline (basically filling in the skeletal outline that you created in Step 2) and placing anything else that you deem important in the reading, directly in your topic outline, should happen in the same sitting for each assigned reading. When you see law students sitting down to "study," they are reading, briefing and outlining at the same time.

STEP 5: BEFORE CLASS

Print the Relevant Portion of Your Outline and Bring It to Class

1. Successful Law Students Do This Skill:

Print the portion of your topic outline that you will cover in class and bring the hardcopy with you to class so you can take notes directly on the hardcopy. If you chose Option 2 in Step 5, print the separate case briefs and bring them to class as well.

2. Successful Law Students' Explanation of How This Skill Leads to an Understanding of Course Material

This skill sets you up for the next step.

3. Successful Law Students' Explanation of How This Skill Equates to Success in the Course

This skill sets you up for the next step.

STEP 6: DURING CLASS

In Class, Confirm Your Understanding of What You Taught Yourself

1. Successful Law Students Do This Skill:

During class, absorb the lecture and interact by:

1. Confirming whether the paragraphs of the case that you translated into your own words are accurate;

2. Confirming whether the rule you pulled in your brief/outline was the correct rule;

3. Confirming whether the rule you translated into your own words is accurate;

4. Taking notes of the professor's cues and what the professor writes on the board;

5. Handwriting on your printed outlines to change/confirm any rule and highlight important facts or professor/student comments; and

6. Confirming whether you can apply or distinguish the rules from the cases to new fact patterns raised by the professor or other students in class.

If you are book briefing, make sure you transfer your lecture notes and rules from your book into your topic outline once they have been confirmed by the professor during lecture.

2. Successful Law Students' Explanation of How This Skill Leads to an Understanding of Course Material

After completing Steps 1–5, you have already *taught yourself* what the professor intends to cover in class. As such, class time is merely a review session, spent verifying whether you learned the material correctly or incorrectly. If you do not learn anything new in class, you truly understand the topics and sub-topics you were assigned that week. This gives you motivation and confidence to continue, knowing you are on the right track. If you learn something new or different in class, you know exactly what topic/sub-topic is unclear, and you must take steps to clarify the confusion. Being able to pinpoint specific areas of confusion (as opposed to feeling like you do not understand the entire course) will make you feel less overwhelmed because you simply need to fix a small topic and move on. Feeling comfortable and confident ultimately leads to a deeper understanding of the material.

3. Successful Law Students Explanation of How This Skill Equates to Success in the Course

If your understanding is confirmed in class or shortly thereafter, you can solidify your rules at that moment and move on to the next topic, knowing that you do not need to spend precious time altering that topic in your topic outline before the midterm or final.

If you did not understand a specific topic or sub-topic in class, spend fifteen minutes after class (don't leave your seat) by reading a supplement, asking a study group partner or grabbing your professor before they leave the podium for clarification.

4. Example

After attending class, your topic outline (which follows the table of contents for that topic) now includes case briefs, notes taken during reading and notes taken in class during the lecture. Your topic outline may look something like Table 11 (following page):

Table 11: Sample Torts Topic Outline

I. INTENTIONAL TORTS (ASSAULT, BATTERY AND INTENTIONAL INFLICTION OF EMOTIONAL DISTRESS [IIED])

  A. Background of Tort Law

    i. Culpability Spectrum in Tort Law (pg. 7)

- People can get in trouble civilly
- Money is form of compensation (also called damages). Different than criminal law where you go to jail.

    ii. Functions and Goals of Negligence Law (pg. 8)

- To protect the public mostly — don't want others harming everyone or being reckless or careless.
- Policy stuff here, [does professor want me to have policy included in my rule statement?]

Discussed problem 2 in class — prof said to pay extra attention to this problem.

    iii. Hot Coffee and Culpability Problems (pg. 13)

Who is responsible for burns? Hot coffee burns, McDonald's case, doughnut case, coffee café place case. How do we satisfy the policy but be careful not to punish everyone??

- Problems with insurance rates going up
- Unaffordability of life basically

    iv. Overview of PI Damages (pg. 27)

Compensatory, punitive and consequential

- Compensatory: to compensate for injury or other loss
- Punitive: to punish someone for recklessness or intentional behavior
- Consequential: the result of someone's bad behavior

Others covered as well but not as big or important as these

    v. Tort Law Litigation Process (pg. 30)

lawsuit, complaint

court, trial, appeal (maybe), judgment

Table 11: Sample Torts Topic Outline *continued*

B. Overview of Intentional Torts (pg. 685)

   1. Assault, Battery and IIED (pg. 686)

   THERE has to be an ACT in the intentional torts (all of them): defined by prof. in class 1 as an overt motion she put this on the board, use this rule)

   Battery = act, intent to cause harmful contact, offensive contact, injury

   2. The Meaning of Intent (pg. 695)

      i. *White v. Muniz* (pg. 695)

      FACTS: An elderly woman who was placed in a personal care center began to exhibit erratic behavior, becoming agitated easily and acting aggressively toward others on occasion. On one occasion, she struck plaintiff caregiver in the jaw. Plaintiff filed a suit for assault and battery, but the court ruled in favor of the elderly woman and her granddaughter. On appeal, the court ruled that a mentally incapacitated adult should be held liable for her intentional tort even if she was unable to appreciate the wrongfulness of her actions. The Supreme Court reversed judgment and reinstated the jury verdict.

      ISSUE: Does an intentional tort require some proof that the tortfeasor not only intended to contact another person, but also intended that the contact be harmful or offensive to the other person?

      RULE: An actor is subject to liability to another for battery if he acts intending to cause a harmful or offensive contact with the person of the other or a third person, or if an imminent apprehension of such a contact, and an offensive or harmful contact with the person of the other directly or indirectly results. An act which is not done with the intention previously stated does not make the actor liable to the other for a mere offensive contact with the other's person although the act involves an unreasonable risk of inflicting it, and therefore, would be negligent or reckless if the risk threatened bodily harm.

      INTENT = desire to cause harmful consequences by her act, although not the harm that actually resulted.

      MY THOUGHTS: this seems logical to me because people should get in trouble if they intend to do something bad.

Table 11: Sample Torts Topic Outline *continued*

ii. *Villa v. Derouen* (pg. 697)

FACTS: Intending only horseplay, D pointed a welding cutting torch in P's direction and intentionally releasing oxygen or acetylene gas and caused unintentional harm to P, i.e., second degree burns to Ps groin area. Under cross-examination, D responded affirmatively when asked if he placed the torch between P's legs and also responded affirmatively when asked if he intended to spray P between the legs with oxygen when he placed the torch between P's legs. Other witnesses testified that D admitted he was playing around with the cutting torch and "goosing" or trying to scare P at the time of the accident.

PROC. HISTORY: Villa (P) appealed from a judgment which held that Derouen (D), a co-employee and his homeowner insurer, were not liable for second-degree burns that P sustained when D intentionally discharged his welding cutting torch near the P's legs

RULE: The jury found that D did not commit an intentional tort against P. This finding foreclosed P from recovery in this action unless it was found that D committed an intentional tort which caused P's injuries. P appealed: the jury erred in finding that D did not commit an intentional tort. —this is because he had the correct intent. If an actor acts and there is a substantial certainty that the result (injury) will happen, then the intent element is satisfied.

REASONING: don't just need to intent to do something—if you know the injury will happen, then that is intent also for this element of battery.

MY THOUGHTS: this also seems fair because the injuries in this case were obvious.

Notes & Questions:

iii. *Doe v. Johnson* (pg. 704)

FACTS: A woman filed a complaint stating several causes of action against a man. The woman claimed that the man was sexually active, engaging in sexual intercourse with multiple partners, prior to having sex with her and, thus, knew or should have known that he had a high risk of becoming infected with the HIV virus because of his sexually

Table 11: Sample Torts Topic Outline *continued*

---

active, promiscuous lifestyle. Thus, the woman claimed that the man had a duty and, in fact, should have warned her of his past lifestyle. The woman further claimed that he did in fact have the HIV virus, and should have either not had sex with her or used a condom.

ISSUE: Is the intent to cause harm to a person required for a defendant to be liable for having caused harm to that person?

RULE: A plaintiff may maintain negligence and fraud claims based on wrongful transmission of venereal diseases, including genital herpes and a defendant's actual knowledge that s/he is infected with an infectious disease is sufficient to establish a duty for purposes of negligence and fraud.

REASONING: There is no need to show that there is intent on the defendant's part to hurt someone. The court determined that the man owed a legal duty to disclose the fact that he might have the HIV virus if he had actual knowledge that he had the HIV virus, had experienced symptoms associated with the HIV virus, or had actual knowledge that a prior sex partner had the HIV virus. The court found that the man owed the woman no duty to disclose that he had engaged in any high-risk activity that increased the odds of carrying or transmitting the HIV virus. It also concluded that strict liability did not apply to the circumstances of this case and that consortium did not apply because no acts were directed at the woman's daughter.

Your topic outline contains *everything* you learned about the topic in one place. See how the cases fit in under the table of contents headings telling you which topic they highlight? See the class notes, the book notes, case briefs and the student's questions? Once you understand all of the cases assigned for the topic, you are done with the topic outline because you will not learn any more information in that topic — you will instead move onto a new topic. All of the completed information on the topic is waiting for you to transform it in Step 7.

STEP 7: AFTER CLASS, AFTER YOU FINISH A TOPIC

Transform the Topic Outline into a Topic Approach

1. Successful Law Students Do This Skill:

Once the topic outline is solidified (meaning you understand the entire topic) and after all of the class sessions on that topic, you need to condense your topic outline down, weeding out any information, bullet points, incomplete sentences or words that will not transfer to an essay when you write that topic on an exam. The condensed topic outline is transformed into a topic approach for the essay. To complete the topic approach, you must go line by line through the topic outline, deciding which information is relevant for the exam and leaving out information that you would not include for that topic on the exam. You have to carefully decide the verbiage for headings and sub-headings in the topic approach, synthesizing umbrella rules, carving out sub-rules and exceptions and creating connector sentences so the bullet points and sentences in the topic outline flow grammatically in the topic approach and when you write them on the exam.

2. Successful Law Students' Explanation of How This Skill Leads to an Understanding of Course Material

The topic approach is a document that allows you to visualize exactly how you will write every topic you could potentially be tested on, in the exam. The rule statements have been verified as correct in class (or after class, if you learned new information in class and had to clarify the rules after class) which gives you motivation and confidence to now start writing practice hypotheticals and problems on the issues you have completed up to that point in the semester.

3. Successful Law Students' Explanation of How This Skill Equates to Success in the Course

Completing the topic approach throughout the semester, after each issue is covered and concluded in class, means you do not have to do anything else with that topic before the final exam. Having a topic approach done after you finish learning about it in class provides you ample time before the midterm and final to simply memorize the topic approach (which will take significantly less time to memorize because you already understand the material) and practice writing the topic. Having a topic approach pre-drafted before the exam saves you from having to think about how you will write the topic, its headings and the rules on the exam, leaving more time for analysis.

4. Examples

Your Torts topic outline for battery may look like Table 12 (following page) after class (this is a very condensed topic outline for purposes of this example but notice how it follows the table of contents and includes case briefs, book notes and lecture notes):

Table 12: Sample Topic Outline for Battery

Intentional Torts

   A. Battery (someone gets physically hurt) covered in week 2 [pgs. 301-49]

- Prof. talked about policy behind battery = we don't want everyone fighting
- This is highly testable

Restatement says: actor liable if [acts] [intending to cause] a [harmful or offensive] [contact] and the other [person gets hurt]

- Prof said these are all elements of battery – we have to deconstruct each element and that's how you'll write it on exam.
  - ○ Intent
    - i. *Pearson v. Chops*:
      - Facts: hit over head to hurt person he did not like
      - Rule: intent is desire for result or substant. cert. of result

Outcome: Yes, intent (I think this was a good result)

  - ○ Harmful/Offensive (reasonable person std.)

Prof said could be either one, don't need to satisfy both for this element.

    - i. *Bunny v. Thompson*: smoke in face is offensive b/c not a smoker
    - ii. *Logan v. Sanders*: throwing knife in face is harmful b/c got hurt
  - ○ Contact (direct or indirect) either one, not both

Two cases with yes contact outcome — one case in the notes & Problems on page 335. Lazer in eye hypo; water spraying from nozzle example in class

Prof= most cases are direct (why?)

  - ○ Injury (normal pi damages) diff rule for punitive if reckless

The Torts topic approach for battery, however, will look like Table 13:

Table 13: Sample Topic Approach for Battery

Battery

A person is liable to another for battery if the person acts, intending to cause a harmful or offensive contact and such contact occurs and causes injury.

Act

An act is an overt motion.

Intent

Intent is acting with a desire to bring a result or acting with a substantial certainty that the result is likely to occur.

Harmful/Offensive Contact

Harmful contact is one that injures a person and an offensive contact is that which a reasonable person finds objectionable.

Contact

Contact can be direct or indirect.

Injury

An injury occurs when a person receives a physical detriment.

As you can see, the topic approach is clear, concise and easy to memorize. Some students also add in case facts or reasoning they learned in each of the sub-topics to help them remember how to apply the case on the final exam.

5. Lisa's Quick Tip

This is the most difficult step in law school. If you struggle with it, that is normal. This step is vital because touching every word in your topic outline and making decisions about the importance of each word forces you to *under-stand* how each sub-topic fits within the larger topic.

To give you an example of the importance of creating a Topic Approach, assume Table 14 is a hypothetical on your midterm:

Table 14: Sample Midterm Hypothetical

The weekend work retreat was the perfect opportunity, Larry figured, to get even with his rival Morgan. "Hey, Morgan, I was grabbing tea for myself. Would you like one, too?" Larry said, holding out a cup of tea, offering it to Morgan. "Gee, thanks, Larry," said Morgan, taking the cup.

Little did Morgan know Larry had swabbed the outside of the cup with a solution of streptococcal bacteria—the pathogen that causes the painful infection known as strep throat. Morgan took the cup and had a sip.

Three days later, he came down with a horrible case of strep throat, which he contracted from Larry's contamination of the cup. Morgan sued Larry for battery.

Discuss whether Larry possessed the requisite intent for battery.

Take a look at Table 15 (Topic Outline) and Table 16 (Topic Approach)—which helps you immediately answer the call of the question in Table 14?

Table 15: Sample Topic Outline for Battery (Condensed)

Intentional Torts

A. Battery (someone gets physically hurt) covered in week 2 [pgs. 301-49]
   • Prof. talked about policy behind battery = we don't want everyone fighting
   • This is highly testable

Restatement says: actor liable if acts intending to cause a harmful or offensive contact and the other person gets hurt

   • Prof said these are all elements of battery—we have to deconstruct each element and that's how you'll write it on exam.
      ◦ Intent
         i. *Pearson v. Chops*:

Facts: hit over head to hurt person he did not like

Table 15: Sample Topic Outline for Battery (Condensed) *continued*

Rule: intent is desire for result or substant. cert. of result

Outcome: Yes, intent (I think this was a good result)

- Harmful/Offensive (reasonable person std.)

Prof said could be either one, don't need to satisfy both for this element.

   i. *Bunny v. Thompson*: smoke in face is offensive b/c not a smoker

   ii. *Logan v. Sanders*: throwing knife in face is harmful b/c got hurt

- Contact (direct or indirect) either one, not both

Two cases with yes contact outcome — one case in the notes & Problems on page 335. Lazer in eye hypo; water spraying from nozzle example in class

Prof= most cases are direct (why?)

- Injury (normal pi damages) diff rule for punitive if reckless

Table 16: Sample Topic Approach for Battery (Condensed)

Battery
A person is liable to another for battery if the person acts, intending to cause a harmful or offensive contact and such contact occurs and causes injury.

Act
An act is an overt motion.

Intent
Intent is acting with a desire to bring a result or acting with a substantial certainty that the result is likely to occur.

Harmful/Offensive Contact
Harmful contact is one that injures a person and an offensive contact is that which a reasonable person finds objectionable.

Contact
Contact can be direct or indirect.

Injury
An injury occurs when a person receives a physical detriment.

Even with just a simple glance, the answer is clear: the topic approach (Table 16) helps you answer the call of the question. Why? Because you don't have to spend any time going through all of the bullet points, cases, and incomplete sentences in the topic outline. You've already spent time reviewing every piece of information you learned on the sub-topic of intent, and you have a clear, concise rule in the topic approach.

If you simply memorized the topic outline and did nothing more, it would be difficult to answer the call of the question because the intent rule is buried — it has not been extrapolated from the topic outline, cases, notes and lecture notes. However, if you created the topic approach, you would have a clear intent rule memorized, understand how it fits into the larger topic of battery and would be able to easily write something like this:

Table 17: Sample Answer to Sample Midterm Hypothetical

> _**Morgan v. Larry**_: Battery (Intent only)
>
> Intent is acting with a desire to bring a result or acting with a substantial certainty that the result is likely to occur.
>
> _The fact that Larry put a highly contagious bacterial strain of streptococcal bacteria on a cup that he gave to Morgan to drink, shows that Larry intended for Morgan to come down with a horrible case of strep throat because he offered it to Morgan, knowing he would drink it._
>
> _Also, Larry acted with substantial certainty that Morgan would get sick because he put a contagious bacteria on a cup that he knew would come in contact with Larry's mouth._
>
> Therefore, Larry possessed the requisite intent for battery.

Having the rule memorized from the topic approach will leave ample time to write the analysis (everything in italic font in Table 17). The analysis is where you will receive the most points from your professor.

The reason Step 7 is difficult for some students is: when combing through their outlines, students are sometimes uncomfortable picking which information transfers to the topic approach and which does not. The topic approach may be too dense if they transfer everything (defeating the purpose of creating the topic approach), and it may be too thin if they don't transfer enough information from the topic outline.

A good rule of thumb, though, is to always refer back to the one-page topic list you created in Step 2 (Table 6) for the first five weeks of Torts I:

Table 6: Sample List of Topics from Syllabus

Intro to Tort Law

Intro to Intent

Intentional Torts

    Intent

    Battery

    Assault

    Intentional Infliction of Emotional Distress

    False Imprisonment

    Trespass

    Trespass to Chattels

    Conversion

Privileges

    Consent

    Self Defense

    Necessity

Just seeing all of the topics in one place makes the task of creating the topic approach much less daunting. Ground yourself. Take out a highlighter and place a box around each sub-topic so you can see how many exist in the topic outline. Then ask yourself the following questions:

- What specific topic am I transforming from the outline into an approach?
- How many pages did this topic cover in the table of contents?
- Does the table of contents for this topic help me understand all of its sub-topics?
- Does my topic outline help me understand all of the sub-topics?

- Can I look at a supplement to understand all of the sub-topics? The rules?
- Do my study partners have the same sub-topics for each main topic?
- What cases did I read for the main topic and its sub-topics?
- Why were each of the cases selected for this topic?
- What was the outcome of each case (i.e., yes intent, no intent, etc.)?
- Do my study partners and I have the same topic approach or are they organized differently? Why?

After you complete the topic approach, you will fully understand the course material and will feel confident writing that topic in practice or on a real exam. Any exam!

STEP 8: AFTER CLASS AND AFTER YOU CREATE A TOPIC APPROACH

Write Practice Essays Using Your Topic Approaches

1. Successful Law Students Do This Skill:

Write three to five hypotheticals, problems in the book and/or short essays for each main topic, using the topic approaches you created in Step 7. Do this throughout the semester, every time you complete a topic outline and transform the topic outline into a topic approach. Do not wait until the last minute to write the practice problems, when your professor's office hours are all booked.

2. Successful Law Students' Explanation of How This Skill Leads to an Understanding of Course Material

At this point, the deep understanding of the topic has already occurred in Step 7, and you are now putting your deep understanding to the test for the first time. Writing practice exams with the topic approaches allows students to visualize and experience how they will approach the topic on an essay midterm or final. Using the topic approach also allows you to determine, before the midterm and final, if the way you anticipate writing the topic flows or if it is awkward on paper.

3. Successful Law Students' Explanation of How This Skill Equates to Success in the Course

If you implement and write with your topic approach enough times before the exam, you will be comfortable using it with any new set of facts you have to apply to your topic approach. You are now ready to write any and all topics, no matter what your professor throws at you for the exam. You can't wait to write the exam because you know the topics so well.

4. Lisa's Quick Tip

Every new hypothetical, problem, practice essay or sample answer you write (using your topic approach) may require you to make small tweaks to your topic approach, ultimately making you happier with your finished work product. That's okay — the topic approach is a fluid document. You know your topic approach is complete when you are able to take and answer any practice problem with the topic approach.

STEP 9: AFTER CLASS AND AFTER YOU FINISH A TOPIC APPROACH

Get Feedback from Your Professor and Study Group to Solidify Your Topic Approach

1. Successful Law Students Do This Skill:

Take or submit a minimum of one to three practice hypotheticals, problems or essays per topic (that you wrote using your topic approach) to your professor for feedback. Implement any feedback about your topic approach organization or rule statements into the issue approaches.

2. Successful Law Students' Explanation of How This Skill Leads to an Understanding of Course Material

For the first time, you now have a rubber stamp of approval that all of your hard work and dedication is now endorsed by your professor. At this point, there is no misunderstanding of the material; you are ready to implement the topic approaches with any fact pattern.

3. Successful Law Students' Explanation of How This Skill Equates to Success in the Course

Now, you can honestly state that you did everything within your power to succeed in your law school course. With the professor having seen and critiqued a minimum of one to three practice exams per issue (allowing you to showcase every topic approach you intend to write on the exam) your confidence will skyrocket through the roof.

4. Lisa's Quick Tip

If you have five topics in one course, you should write a minimum of approximately 15 practice problems (5 topics multiplied by 3 practice problems per topic) before the final exam. Knowing the number of topics in your course and knowing when you will be done learning everything about them during the semester helps you plan your weekly calendar, which is explained in Chapter 3.

How much more confident can you be walking into an exam with a deep understanding of and approach for writing every topic you could possibly be tested on, having practiced writing every topic and *also having your professor approve or give invaluable feedback on your writing of each topic*? You can walk into any exam knowing there is nothing more that you could have done to prepare for the exam — this is the most gratifying feeling you will experience in your entire law school career.

Conclusion

Table 18 is a visual of the nine-step successful law school study process you just read about:

Table 18: Visual of the Nine-Step Successful Law School Study Process:

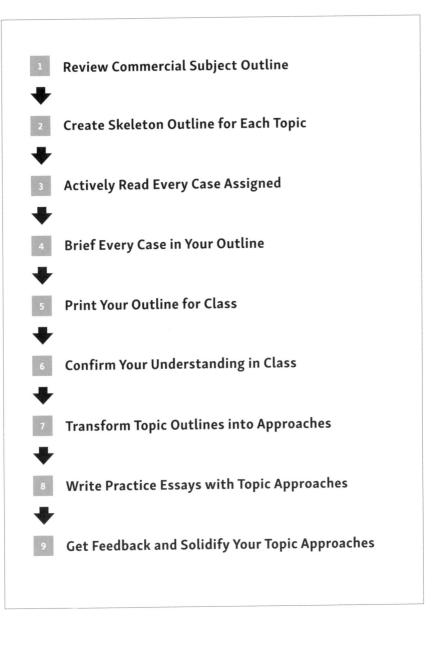

1. Review Commercial Subject Outline

2. Create Skeleton Outline for Each Topic

3. Actively Read Every Case Assigned

4. Brief Every Case in Your Outline

5. Print Your Outline for Class

6. Confirm Your Understanding in Class

7. Transform Topic Outlines into Approaches

8. Write Practice Essays with Topic Approaches

9. Get Feedback and Solidify Your Topic Approaches

The last piece of the successful study process is how to schedule each study step every week to ensure you stay at least one week ahead in each of your classes. Chapter 3 explains how to implement the study process into a weekly schedule.

CHAPTER THREE

Implementing the Nine-Step Study Process into a Weekly Schedule

The study participants agree that the best way to relieve law school anxiety is to create a list of tasks in every subject. Doing so allows you to know how much work you have each week and to decide when and where you will complete each of your study tasks. Since law professors assign weekly reading, it makes sense to place your law school tasks into a weekly calendar.

Students without a study process don't always see the need for calendaring because they do not have clearly identified study tasks or goals. What we learned from Chapter 1 and 2 though, is that there are several skills included in the successful study process, and if we fail to organize them into a completion timeline or schedule, they will be meaningless.

Since calendaring may be a new skill for some let's start basic — with a pen and paper — so you have a physical rendering of how packed your semester weeks will become after you input all of your necessary study steps. I know many students are not accustomed to using a handwritten calendar. If you are opposed to doing so, please trust me on this and just try to physically write out *one week* of your semester. You need a tangible understanding of what a week will look like (as opposed to scrolling through a tiny screen) to understand the importance of doing it for the remaining weeks of your semester. Once you master scheduling and start completing the tasks in your written schedule on autopilot, feel free to use any and all technology (and its awesome reminders) to calendar your weekly study steps.

Start by printing a weekly calendar for every week of your semester. For example, if there are fourteen weeks in your semester, you need fourteen weekly calendars. As seen in Table 19, along the left rows, there should be hours from 7am to 11pm and there should be seven columns for each day of the week, Sunday through Saturday.

Table 19: Sample Weekly Calendar

	SUN.	MON.	TUES.	WED.	THURS.	FRI.	SAT.
7a							
8a							
9a							
10a							
11a							
12p							
1p							
2p							
3p							
4p							
5p							
6p							
7p							
8p							
9p							
10p							
11p							

Grab several different colored highlighters and a pen and do the following:

1. In pen, draw a block of time for the hours you have to work, if any.

2. In pen, draw a block of time for each of your classes and label the blocks with your class subject.

3. Pull out your syllabi and look to see what the reading is for each week (this is Step 2 of the nine-step successful study process).

4. Decide which day(s) you will complete the weekly assigned reading, briefing and topic outlining for each subject. Use one highlighter to indicate this block of time is for reading, briefing and topic outlining. Be

sure to include the specific page numbers assigned in each class so you allocate enough time to complete the task.

5. Add in a block of time to review your printed outlines (that you printed in Step 5 of the nine-step successful study process) *before class*, for fifteen minutes. Use a red marker to indicate these time blocks.

6. Add in a block of time to modify, add or delete (if needed) comments you made on the printed topic outline to the same topic outline in your computer *after class* to reflect what you learned during class. Use the same red marker to outline these blocks, indicating you are doing a post-class review of your topic outline.

7. Add in a block of time to transform the topic outlines into topic approaches (this is Step 7 in the nine-step successful study process) after you have completed a topic (this requires you to know which weeks you finish topics so you can schedule this skill in those weeks). Pick one color highlighter for these time blocks so you know which task you are completing.

8. Add in a block of time to practice writing hypotheticals, practice essays and problems in your book, using your topic approach for each topic (this also requires you to know which weeks in your semester you finish topics so you can schedule this skill in on those weeks). Pick one color highlighter for these time blocks so you know which task you are completing.

9. Add in time to practice multiple choice questions if your professor has them on the midterm or final exam. Pick one color highlighter for these time blocks so you know which skill you are completing.

10. Add in time for exercise, personal time, self-care. Pick one color highlighter for these time blocks so you know when you can relax and enjoy your beautiful life a little.

11. Add in time for family and friends. Pick one color highlighter for these time blocks so you know when you can relax and enjoy your beautiful and precious life.

12. Now, scan and email your weekly or semester-long schedule to everyone you know so they can see what your life will look like in the fall or spring. This helps them cut you a little slack but, more importantly, lets them know when they can expect to have time with you.

Table 20 is a sample weekly schedule (without the various highlighted colors) for a full-time student who does not work.

Each of the nine-steps have been incorporated into the below sample weekly schedule for a full-time student. The few darkened blocks are your free time.

Table 20: Sample Full-Time Student Weekly Calendar

	SUNDAY	MONDAY	TUESDAY
7a	Go for Run		Yoga Class
8a	Practice Torts Multiple-Choice		
9a		Torts Class	Review Property Printed Outline
10a			
11a	Read, brief and outline for Real Property	Review Contracts printed outline	Real Property Class
12p		Contracts Class	
1p			Sit outside in the sun
2p		Modify, if needed Torts and Contracts Outline	
3p	Pg. 1–65		
4p			
5p		Read, brief and outline for Torts	Review Crim Printed Outline
6p			
7p		Page 4–32; 115–154	
8p			Criminal Law Class
9p		Go for Run	
10p	Review Torts printed outline		
11p			

WEDNESDAY	THURSDAY	FRIDAY	SATURDAY
		Yoga Class	
Review Torts printed outline			Practice K Multiple-Choice
Torts Class	Review Property Printed Outline		
Review Contracts printed outline	Real Property Class	Legal Writing & Research Class	
Contracts Class			
	Modify, if needed, Real Property, and Criminal Law Outlines		Read, brief and outline for Contracts
Read for Legal Writing & Research			Pg. 20–46; 52–70
Pg. 29–46; 80–91	Write Battery Hypo		
		Read, brief and outline for Criminal Law	
	Friend/ Family Dinner Night	Pg. 70–112; 48–60	
Transform Battery Outline to Approach			Meet friends for coffee

I recommend large blocks of time for the task of reading, briefing and outlining, with no classes scheduled after that block because you should continue until you finish that task. Don't go to bed until that task is completed. In the beginning, the reading, briefing and outlining will take longer to complete and maybe even longer than you scheduled. That's normal. Some weeks you will get more sleep and some less. Just make sure you do not move onto the next week without completing the tasks you have scheduled in the prior week because you will lose your critical study motivation, discussed in Chapter 1.

If sitting for large periods of time does not work for you, schedule a block of time to stand up and get your blood flowing every hour. If you cannot work on one subject for an entire task block, split the block into chunks where you work on several subjects in that time block — just be sure to incorporate all of the reading for each subject amongst the blocks of your week.

Table 21 is a sample weekly schedule (without the various highlighted colors) for a part-time student who works.

Table 21: Sample Part-Time Student Weekly Calendar

	SUN.	MON.	TUES.	WED.	THURS.	FRI.	SAT.
7a							
8a	Go for Run						
9a							
10a	Transform Battery Outline to Approach						Write Battery Hypo
11a							
12p		Work	Work	Work	Work	Work	
1p							
2p							
3p							Read, brief and outline for Criminal Law
4p	Read, brief and outline for Torts						
5p							
6p	Page 4–32; 115–154	Review Torts Printed Outline	Go for Run	Review Crim Printed Outline		Yoga Class	Pg. 70–112; 48–60
7p	Practice Torts Multiple-Choice	Torts Class	Read for Legal Writing & Research Pg. 29–46; 80–91	Criminal Law Class	Legal Research & Writing Class	Practice Crim Multiple-Choice Modify, if needed, Torts, and Criminal Law Outlines	Friend/ Family Dinner Night
8p							
9p	Meet friends for coffee						
10p							
11p							

Stay One Week (or More) Ahead of Your Assigned Reading

You should be able to access your syllabi from your law school website or Admissions Department a minimum of one week before your semester begins. You should spend that week before classes completing Steps 1 through 9 for each class. If you have your syllabi earlier, you can start Steps 1 through 9 earlier because *Nine Steps* will walk you through the study process and motivate you to do the work. Some law students prefer to be two to three weeks ahead of the assigned reading. Other students read fifteen pages per subject every day, following the *Nine Steps* process for each class.

Staying ahead in your reading allows you to tend to unforeseen life events or to take an entire week before midterms to complete Steps 8 and 9.

Law Students with Children

If you have children, I recommend creating one block of time every day where you devote undivided attention to your kids, no matter what their age (newborn to eighteen). Tell your kids you value them, and that law school is a personal goal of yours that will allow you to help people and make positive changes in the world. Encourage them to support your dream. Remind them how much you love them with random notes (or scavenger hunts) or writing on their bathroom mirror or a note on your fridge. Tell them they are so important that you have carved out a time for them every day where there are no cell phones, computers or outside influences. Make your daily block memorable by preparing or eating a family meal, doing a special craft every morning, reading books in a fort after lunch, a bed-time routine — anything you can do to make your child feel a part of your life despite your busy schedule.

If you keep their attention tanks full and remind them how much you eagerly anticipate their block of time every day you will still feel connected despite your work and law school life.

Conclusion

Sometimes just seeing the above sample weekly schedule makes students feel nauseous. Try not to let it get the better of you, and instead let your calendar make you feel in control of your life. Read Chapter 4 for a few paragraphs of inspiration as you prepare for law school!

CHAPTER FOUR

Chop the Wood in Front of You

The next sentence may surprise you.

At the beginning of your semester, *your goal in law school should not be to get a 4.0 in your law school classes.* The 4.0 grade is a random, often-times subjective number that will be assigned to you by your professor in fourteen short weeks. If you continue telling yourself that law school success is measured by the grade at the end, you've missed the point of *Nine Steps*, you won't sleep at night, you'll feel unnecessary stress and you won't be happy. That's because the end result — that 4.0 grade — is not within your control at the outset of your studies.

What *is in your control*, though, is what you do every day leading up to the midterm and final exam. You are 100% in control of completing the tasks you schedule every day in your weekly calendar. You are 100% in control of the effort and passion you put into studying. You are 100% in control of your adult-law-student-self and the decisions you make every moment.

Since the study in this book scientifically proves that grit elevates intellect (and not the other way around) *your goal in law school should be to complete the tasks you've scheduled for yourself on a daily basis.* If you complete the tasks you've assigned yourself every day, you will rest soundly at night, knowing you did what you were supposed to do in the limited space of the day. As those days culminate into weeks, and weeks into the fourteen-week semester, you can honestly walk into the final exam and confidently say, "*I did everything possible that I could do to succeed on this exam.*"

If you can genuinely say that to yourself, you won't care about the grade you receive in the class because you gave everything of yourself to succeed. Regardless of your grade, there is no greater feeling of accomplishment before taking a final exam. You should be reading this and telling yourself, "I have that feeling, I am ready to take my able-minded self and go get after it!"

Right now, go find a piece of paper and write the words: "Today I will succeed because I will give 100%." Tape that lovely piece of paper above your desk so you are reminded of the passion you possess to succeed, which will get you through the grueling days of law school. Add a simple mark to it on tough law school days and you will find, with a little grit, those marks will occur less frequently.

Knowing what is in your control, chop only the wood in front of you. The rest will be there tomorrow with the other neatly arranged daily stacks, waiting patiently for you to unravel them.

Quick Template for Conducting Qualitative Phenomenological Research

1. Figure out the specific phenomenon you want to uncover.

2. Understand the definition of qualitative research to ensure it is the proper approach to conduct your research.

   a. If not, the other option is quantitative research.

3. Understand the definition of the phenomenological scientific methodology to ensure it is the proper methodology to allow you to uncover your phenomenon.

   a. If not, the other main scientific methodologies are ethnography, grounded-theory, narrative research and case study.

4. Select your research participants by using one of the following techniques:

   a. Convenience Sample

   b. Theoretical Sample

   c. Judgment Sample (used in *Nine Steps*)

5. Collect your study data by using one of the following data collection methods:

   a. Interview (used in *Nine Steps*)

   b. Observation

   c. Written Documents (used in *Nine Steps*)

6. Interpret your study data.

7. Write a composite summary of your data.

8. Discover and interpret themes within your data.

Successful Study Process
Quick Reference Table

STEP 1	Find and read subject-specific commercial outlines, outlines from other students who took the course with the same professor or outlines from students who took the course with a different professor.
STEP 2	Open your syllabus and review the reading the professor has assigned for the semester, paying close attention to how the professor organized the topics and sub-topics.
	Next, write down a list of the main topics (as written in the syllabus) you are responsible for learning all semester.
	Then, open your textbook table of contents and view the table of contents for the pages assigned in the syllabus.
	Finally, open a word document and create a skeleton outline that mirrors the table of contents for the pages you are assigned to read. Create one outline, for each main topic, that includes the headings, sub-headings and case names as they are listed and appear in the table of contents.
STEP 3	Read every case assigned in the syllabus each week, every week. Don't fall behind the syllabus. For every paragraph of the decision, translate what occurred in your own words and/or with drawings. Write your translations in the margin of your textbook.

continued on next page

continued

STEP 4	Pick one of the following options:
	Option 1: Brief every case you read directly in your skeletal outline. Ask yourself why the author of your textbook included the case in the chapter under the heading/sub-heading it falls under in the table of contents. Narrow the rule by determining which facts, policy or circumstance the case was decided upon. Re-write the rule of each case in your own words.
	Option 2: Brief every case and place the brief into a document separate from your skeletal outline. Ask yourself why the author of your textbook included the case in the chapter under the heading/sub-heading within which it falls. Narrow the rule by determining which facts, policy or circumstance the case was decided upon. Re-write the rule of each case in your own words.
	Option 3: Book brief every case you read. Narrow the rule by determining which facts, policy or circumstance the case was decided upon. Re-write the rule of each case in your own words.
STEP 5	Print the portion of your topic outline that you will cover in class and bring the hardcopy with you to class so you can take notes directly on the hardcopy. If you chose Option 2 in Step 5, print the separate case briefs, and bring them to class as well.
STEP 6	During class, absorb the lecture and interact by:
	1. Confirming whether the paragraphs of the case that you translated into your own words are accurate;
	2. Confirming whether the rule you pulled in your brief/outline was the correct rule;
	3. Confirming whether the rule you translated into your own words is accurate;
	4. Taking notes of the professor's cues and what the professor writes on the board;
	5. Handwriting on your printed outlines to change/confirm any rule and highlight important facts or professor/student comments; and
	6. Confirming whether you can apply or distinguish the rules from the cases to new fact patterns raised by the professor or other students in class.
	If you are book briefing, make sure you transfer your lecture notes and rules from your book into your topic outline once they have been confirmed by the professor during lecture.

STEP 7	Once the topic outline is solidified (meaning you understand the entire topic) and after all of the class sessions on that topic, you need to condense your topic outline down, weeding out any information, bullet points, incomplete sentences or words that will not transfer to an essay when you write that topic on an exam. The condensed topic outline is transformed into a topic approach for the essay. To complete the topic approach, you must go line by line through the topic outline, deciding which information is relevant for the exam and leaving out information that you would not include for that topic on the exam. You have to carefully decide the verbiage for headings and sub-headings in the topic approach, synthesizing umbrella rules, carving out sub-rules and exceptions and creating connector sentences so the bullet points and sentences in the topic outline flow grammatically in the topic approach and when you write them on the exam.
STEP 8	Write three to five hypotheticals, problems in the book and/or short essays for each main topic, using the topic approaches you created in Step 7. Do this throughout the semester, every time you complete a topic outline and transform the topic outline into a topic approach. Do not wait until the last minute to write the practice problems, when your professor's office hours are all booked.
STEP 9	Take or submit a minimum of one to three practice hypotheticals, problems or essays per topic (that you wrote using your topic approach) to your professor for feedback. Implement any feedback about your topic approach organization or rule statements into the issue approaches.

Successful Study Process with Explanations Quick Reference Table

Before the Semester Starts	**BEFORE CLASS**	**STEP 1**	Successful Law Students Do This Skill (1 hour)	Find and read subject-specific commercial outlines, outlines from other students who took the course with the same professor or outlines from students who took the course with a different professor.
			Successful Law Students' Explanation of How This Skill Leads to an Understanding of Material	This skill provides you with a big picture of all of the main topics and sub-topics covered in a course so you can visualize the relationships (or lack thereof) between the topics and sub-topics and understand the totality of what you might learn when the semester begins.
			Successful Law Students' Explanation of How This Skill Equates to Success in the Course	This step provides you with an all-inclusive framework of the subject, without the pressure of having to understand every intricate piece. It makes every subsequent step in the study process easier because you will have already reviewed the topics in the subject once. and each new topic won't appear as daunting on its second read. It's comforting to read something you already know about.
		STEP 2	Successful Law Students Do This Skill (1 hour)	Open your syllabus and review the reading the professor has assigned for the semester, paying close attention to how the professor organized the topics and sub-topics.
				Next, write down a list of the main topics (as written in the syllabus) you are responsible for learning all semester.
				Then, open your textbook table of contents and view the table of contents for the pages assigned in the syllabus.
				Finally, open a Word Document and create a skeleton outline that mirrors the table of contents for the pages you are assigned to read. Create one outline for each main topic that includes the headings, sub-headings and case names as they are listed and appear in the table of contents.

Before the Semester Starts	**STEP 2** *(continued)*	Successful Law Students' Explanation of How This Skill Leads to an Understanding of Material	This skill provides a detailed frame of main topics and sub-topics that your professor expects you to master. It also allows you to categorize topics and chunk very specific information that you must learn within each topic. Although this step requires no substantive knowledge, it provides confidence at the beginning of the semester because you have touched and organized each of the main and sub-topics before the semester begins. You are then aware of exactly how many issues you will learn, which makes the course feel more "doable."
		Successful Law Students' Explanation of How This Skill Equates to Success in the Course	If you grasp from the outset that there are main topics, which are comprised of several sub-topics, you are more likely to: (1) separate the main issues when you write a midterm or final exam; (2) understand which parts of the sub-issues are relevant and irrelevant to the fact pattern (saving time to focus analysis on the proper issues during the exam); (3) follow IRAC for each topic and its sub-topics; and (4) apply the correct facts to the correct topic/sub-topic.
During the Semester	**BEFORE CLASS** · **STEP 3**	Successful Law Students Do This Skill (As long as it takes to finish the assigned reading)	Read every case assigned in the syllabus each week, every week. Don't fall behind the syllabus. For every paragraph of the decision, translate what occurred in your own words and/or with drawings. Write your translations in the margin of your textbook.
		Successful Law Students' Explanation of How This Skill Leads to an Understanding of Material	This step requires you to monitor your own understanding of the material. It forces you to be present and focused while reading difficult material. If you cannot translate the material into your own words, that is a cue that you *do not understand the material* and must then determine what needs to be done in that exact moment to ensure you meet the goal of understanding the legal issue raised in the case.
		Successful Law Students' Explanation of How This Skill Equates to Success in the Course	If you understand what you are reading in the moment, you will be more engaged in class because you won't be confused and can instead follow along. You will be excited for the professor to call on you in class so you can showcase what you taught yourself. Monitoring your knowledge allows for you to spend far less time memorizing immediately before a midterm or final, leaving ample time for more critical writing practice before the midterm or final.

During the Semester	BEFORE CLASS	STEP 4		
			Successful Law Students Do This Skill (Pick One)	**Option 1:** Brief every case you read directly in your skeletal outline. Ask yourself why the author of your textbook included the case in the chapter under the heading/sub-heading it falls under in the table of contents. Narrow the rule by determining which facts, policy or circumstance the case was decided upon. Rewrite the rule of each case in your own words. **OR;** **Option 2:** Brief every case and place the brief into a document separate from your skeletal outline. Ask yourself why the author of your textbook included the case in the chapter under the heading/sub-heading within which it falls. Narrow the rule by determining which facts, policy or circumstance the case was decided upon. Rewrite the rule of each case in your own words. **OR;** **Option 3:** Book brief every case you read. Narrow the rule by determining which facts, policy or circumstance the case was decided upon. Rewrite the rule of each case in your own words.
			Successful Law Students' Explanation of How This Skill Leads to an Understanding of Material	Briefing forces you to distill the most important parts of the case. Placing the brief into your topic outline allows you to visualize the topics and sub-topics that the author of the textbook thought required a case to illuminate a particular issue or an interesting factual scenario. You can also see where the points will be on the exam because if there are seven cases on one topic but only one on another, that's a hint that the topic with more cases is important. Narrowing the rule forces you to boil the case down to the specific fact(s) the case was decided upon. Doing so allows you to see which facts are integral to the decision and which facts your professor might "play with" in terms of testing whether the case would have the same outcome should different facts apply.
			Successful Law Students' Explanation of How This Skill Equates to Success in the Course	Briefing cases while outlining and reading simultaneously forces you to cover and prepare everything in one place, at one time. The topic outlines contain every piece of information the student needs to know (minus step 6) for each topic and all of its sub-topics on the midterm and final exam. This is important because when it comes time to transform the outlines in step 7 (the most important step), you will not waste time flipping through several documents (that do not follow the table of contents or syllabus) in an effort to synthesize the materials. Reading, briefing and outlining every week as you read saves time for critical thinking in class and saves coveted time before midterms and finals to practice writing.

During the Semester			
	IN CLASS	STEP 5	Successful Law Students Do This Skill (2 minutes)	Print the portion of your topic outline that you will cover in class and bring the hardcopy with you to class so you can take notes directly on the hardcopy. If you chose Option 2 in Step 5, print the separate case briefs, and bring them to class as well.
			Successful Law Students' Explanation of How This Skill Leads to an Understanding of Material	This skill sets you up for the next step.
			Successful Law Students' Explanation of How This Skill Equates to Success in the Course	This skill sets you up for the next step.
		STEP 6	Successful Law Students Do This Skill (Pick one)	During class, absorb the lecture and interact by: (1) Confirming whether the paragraphs of the case that you translated into your own words are accurate; (2) Confirming whether the rule you pulled in your brief/outline was the correct rule; (3) Confirming whether the rule you translated into your own words is accurate; (4) Taking notes of the professor's cues and what the professor writes on the board; (5) Handwriting on your printed outlines to change/confirm any rule and highlight important facts or professor/student comments; and (6) Confirming whether you can apply or distinguish the rules from the cases to new fact patterns raised by the professor or other students in class. **OR;** If you are book briefing make sure you transfer your lecture notes and rules from your book into your topic outline once they have been confirmed by the professor during lecture.

During the Semester			
	IN CLASS	STEP 6 (continued)	Successful Law Students' Explanation of How This Skill Leads to an Understanding of Material	After completing steps 1–5, you have already taught yourself what the professor intends to cover in class. As such, class time is merely a review session, spent verifying whether you learned the material correctly or incorrectly. If you do not learn anything new in class, you truly understand the topics and sub-topics you were assigned that week. This gives you motivation and confidence to continue, knowing you are on the right track. If you learn something new or different in class, you know exactly what topic/sub-topic is unclear, and you must take steps to clarify the confusion. Being able to pin-point specific areas of confusion (as opposed to feeling like you do not understand the entire course) will make you feel less overwhelmed because you simply need to fix a small topic and move on. Feeling comfortable and confident ultimately leads to a deeper understanding of the material.
			Successful Law Students' Explanation of How This Skill Equates to Success in the Course	If your understanding is confirmed in class or shortly thereafter, you can solidify your rules at that moment and move on to the next topic, knowing that you do not need to spend precious time altering that topic in your topic outline before the midterm or final.
	AFTER CLASS	STEP 7	Successful Law Students Do This Skill (The Most Important, Time-Consuming and Difficult Skill)	Once the topic outline is solidified (meaning, you understand the entire topic) and after all of the class sessions on that topic, you need to condense your topic outline, weeding out any information, bullet points, incomplete sentences or words that will not transfer to an essay when you write that topic on an exam. The condensed topic outline is transformed into a topic approach for the essay. To complete the topic approach, you must go line by line through the topic outline, deciding which information is relevant for the exam and leaving out information that you would not include for that topic on the exam. You have to carefully decide the verbiage for headings and sub-headings in the topic approach, synthesizing umbrella rules, carving out sub-rules and exceptions and creating connector sentences so the bullet points and sentences in the topic outline flow grammatically in the topic approach and when you write them on the exam.
			Successful Law Students' Explanation of How This Skill Leads to an Understanding of Material	The topic approach is a document that allows you to visualize exactly how you will write every topic you could potentially be tested on in the exam. The rule statements have been verified as correct in class (or after class if you learned new information in class and had to clarify the rules after class), which gives you motivation and confidence to now start writing practice hypos and problems on the issues you have completed up to that point in the semester.

During the Semester	AFTER CLASS	STEP 7 (continued)	Successful Law Students' Explanation How This Skill Equates to Success in the Course	Completing the topic approach throughout the semester after each issue is covered and concluded in class means you do not have to do anything else with that topic before the final exam. Having a topic approach done after you finish learning about it in class provides you ample time before the midterm and final to simply memorize the topic approach (which will take significantly less time to memorize because you already understand the material) and practice writing the topic. Having a topic approach pre-drafted before the exam saves you from having to think about how you will write the topic, its headings and the rules on the exam, leaving more time for analysis.
		STEP 8	Successful Law Students Do This Skill	Write three to five hypotheticals, problems in the book and/or short essays for each main topic, using the topic approaches you created in Step 7. Do this throughout the semester, every time you complete a topic outline and transform the topic outline into a topic approach. Do not wait until the last minute to write the practice problems, when your professor's office hours are all booked.
			Successful Law Students' Explanation of How This Skill Leads to an Understanding of Material	At this point, the deep understanding of the topic has already occurred in Step 7, and you are now putting your deep understanding to the test for the first time. Writing practice exams with the topic approaches allows students to visualize and experience how they will approach the topic on an essay midterm or final. Using the topic approach also allows you to determine, before the midterm and final, if the way you anticipate writing the topic flows or if it is awkward on paper.
			Successful Law Students' Explanation of How This Skill Equates to Success in the Course	If you implement and write with your topic approach enough times before the exam, you will be comfortable using it with any new set of facts you have to apply to your topic approach. You are now ready to write any and all topics, no matter what your professor throws at you for the exam. You can't wait to write the exam because you know the topics so well.

<table>
<tr><td rowspan="3">During the Semester</td><td rowspan="3">AFTER CLASS</td><td rowspan="3">STEP 9</td><td>Successful Law Students Do This Skill</td><td>Take or submit a minimum of one to three practice hypotheticals, problems or essays per topic (that you wrote using your topic approach) to your professor for feedback. Implement any feedback about your topic approach organization or rule statements into the issue approaches.</td></tr>
<tr><td>Successful Law Students' Explanation of How This Skill Leads to an Understanding of Material</td><td>For the first time, you now have a rubber stamp of approval that all of your hard work and dedication is endorsed by your professor. At this point, there is no misunderstanding of the material; you are ready to implement the topic approaches with any fact pattern.</td></tr>
<tr><td>Successful Law Students' Explanation of How This Skill Equates to Success in the Course</td><td>Now, you can honestly state that you did everything within your power to succeed in your law school course. With the professor having seen and critiqued a minimum of one to three practice exams per issue (allowing you to showcase every topic approach you intend to write on the exam) your confidence will skyrocket through the roof.</td></tr>
</table>

Index

Page numbers in *italics* refer to tables.

topic outlines, 4; topic approach derived
from (step 7), 60–68, 75, *93–94. See
also* sub-topics
translation, of cases, 49–50

U
units of meaning, 20, *22–25*

V
validity checks, in survey research, 29

W
weekly calendars, 73–75, *76–77*, 78
work-life balance, 75, 80